H. Coupland Taylor

Wanderings in Search of Health

Or, Medical and meteorological Notes on various Foreign Health Resorts

H. Coupland Taylor

Wanderings in Search of Health
Or, Medical and meteorological Notes on various Foreign Health Resorts

ISBN/EAN: 9783337193850

Printed in Europe, USA, Canada, Australia, Japan

Cover: Foto ©Andreas Hilbeck / pixelio.de

More available books at **www.hansebooks.com**

WANDERINGS IN SEARCH OF HEALTH

WANDERINGS

IN

SEARCH OF HEALTH

OR

MEDICAL AND METEOROLOGICAL NOTES ON VARIOUS FOREIGN HEALTH RESORTS

BY

H. COUPLAND TAYLOR, M.D.

FELLOW OF THE ROYAL METEOROLOGICAL SOCIETY, ETC.

" All is but lip wisdom that wants experience."—SIR PHILIP SIDNEY.

WITH ILLUSTRATIONS

LONDON
H. K. LEWIS, 136 GOWER STREET, W.C.
1890

PRINTED BY
H. K. LEWIS, 136 GOWER STREET,
LONDON, W.C.

Dedicatio.

CONJUGI

MEÆ DILECTISSIMÆ

ITINERUM

PARTI MAGNÆ ET COMITI,

EORUM

HÆC RELICTA

DEDICO.

ILLUSTRATIONS.

WANDERINGS

IN

SEARCH OF HEALTH.

INTRODUCTION.

MANY are the books and monographs on
Health Resorts by medical men possessing
technical knowledge and experience as to
the requirements which such places should
supply. Some are by those who have only
paid a flying visit to the various localities,
and that whilst in health and vigour, and
who therefore can scarcely appreciate their
several advantages and disadvantages to the
invalid ; for it is more especially he who goes
in a weakly condition to recover his health,
who begins to find out and duly appreciate
the merits and faults of any given place.
Again, many monographs of localities are
written by those who have lived and practised in them, and who are therefore uncon-

B

sciously prejudiced in favour of their own
locality, not only from their living in the
place and seeing many of their patients do
well and improve in health, but also from
their owing, very probably, their own re-
stored health to it, therefore they naturally
praise it even beyond its deserts, when it
is brought into comparison with other
places.

It is no doubt hard even for two invalids
to entirely agree on the various advantages
and disadvantages of a health resort, not
only because their maladies and constitutions
differ, but also on account of their inherited
and acquired tastes ; one feeling moped and
bored in a quiet and more or less country
place where there is but little gaiety going
on, while another will feel far happier there,
and far more contented with Nature's surroundings than with the artificial attractions
of a fashionable town with its promenades,
balls and theatres.

Nevertheless most medical men will agree,
more or less entirely at all events, on the
broader points of discussion as to the merits
of a given place, and as to its suitability as

a health-giving locality for various classes of invalids.

Now it is from a medical man's point of view, who himself is an invalid, and who has been abroad for several years in search of health, but who previously had also travelled a good deal in Europe, America and the Colonies in health, that the following pages have been written ; and he has in them, without favour or malice, and he hopes, too, without giving offence, jotted down his personal impressions of, and his experiences in, various localities for the information and guidance of others. Nobody can deny that there is still much room for a fuller and better knowledge of the kind of climate and of the nature of the accommodation and surroundings which invalids and convalescents, who are often indiscriminately sent abroad for change of air, are likely to meet with at foreign resorts. That this is the case amongst not only country practitioners and those who have never had the opportunity of travelling abroad, but also amongst London consultants, is amply proved by many statements made regarding the climate or advantages of some given place, and by the tales of the bitter disappointments and the disagreeable experiences of many an invalid whom one meets abroad.

The plan of advertising new resorts by interested hotel, railway or steamboat companies by means of puffing pamphlets, is a great and growing evil, spreading broadcast, as they so frequently do, most misleading and exaggerated statements, thus causing many of these bitter disappointments.

Again, the diametrically opposing opinions held in one resort as to the climate and merits of another are quite an amusing study. Thus in the Riviera it is said that the Alpine resorts can only be injurious, on account of the long hours patients have to spend indoors in an atmosphere vitiated by hot stoves, and on account of the close contact of so many phthisical patients in rooms where proper ventilation cannot be properly effected, through the great draughts caused by the coldness of the external air in that climate, and its great contrast to the air of the heated rooms. The difference indeed is often 60 degrees. On the other hand, at Davos it is said that the Riviera is all very well for patients who can never expect to recover, and who only want a mitigating climate to die in; but that to expect any consumptive, for instance, to be cured, or obtain any permanent benefit, would be the height of absurdity. Again, in Madeira it is said that the cold winds of the Riviera are most injurious to invalids, and that the glowing descriptions often written on the climate experienced there are merely poetical rhapsodies as applied to the Mediterranean littoral, but if taken literally, do exactly describe the climate of Madeira: that what is euphemistically described as "the invigorating and bracing air" of the Riviera really means, if translated into ordinary language, "cold, wintry and windy weather."

So the battle of health resorts proceeds, each locality being praised and decried in turn, so that it is most difficult to come to a satisfactory conclusion as to the real merits of a place, unless it has been actually

visited and lived in, and due comparison
made with other localities.

The following pages are written primarily
from the point of view of the *poitrinaire*, and
it is with his wants and requirements that
they are chiefly concerned. Nevertheless
other ailments may be referred to, and will
be more especially named when reference to
them is indicated.

With regard to the indiscriminate way in
which patients are sent abroad, which I
have alluded to above, and the sad results
of which, one is constantly coming across,
Dr. Clifford Allbutt has well said, "it is
astounding to see the airy way in which a
doctor, who has never been out of England,
orders off his patients, this one to Aix, that to
Carlsbad, and a third to Davos, and so forth,
merely on the knowledge that one is good
for rheumatism, the second for liver, and the
third for phthisis." Whereas to advise
rightly it requires not only an accurate
knowledge of the precise kind of case to be
sent, but also some knowledge of the characteristics of the locality itself which is
chosen. A knowledge of the mere baro-

metric, thermometric and hygrometric readings of a place are not sufficient, though of
course they are of great value in helping
towards a decision. A personal experience
of the climate, of such a climate as that of
Davos for instance, should be had, if
possible, before a patient who is in at all a
critical condition should be sent there.
Such cases, again, should only be sent away
sparingly from home at all, and by no
means as a matter of course. In no disease
is this knowledge more needed or of so
much importance as in phthisis, for in this
complaint a wrong decision may greatly
aggravate the malady, and instead of an
invalid having all the attention his relations
at home could give him, and would often be
only too glad to give him, he not unfrequently dies away from home amongst
strangers, neglected and uncared for. Such
sad cases are constantly occurring; sometimes indeed the invalids die almost immediately after their arrival, not having sufficient strength even to survive the fatigues of
the journey or voyage. A case very much
to the point has just come under my notice;

the lady in question having been a patient
of a friend of mine. Though her own
medical man was against her leaving home,
she was advised to do so by a consultant.
She was carried from her room to the cab,
from thence into the train, and from thence
on board a steamer for a passage of some
days' duration. On arriving at her destination she was carried up to her bedroom at the
hotel to die, far away from home and amongst
strangers, only four days after her arrival.

It is in the endeavour to change the
entire surroundings and environment of
the patient that the climatic treatment of
phthisis becomes so valuable; thus striking
if possible at the cause which has induced
the disease, whether it be an unhealthy employment, a damp soil, unhygienic surroundings, a vicious mode of life, or what not.
Consumptive patients too generally labour
under the error that they have just a little
"delicacy of the chest," and that a couple of
months' holiday will set them all right again,
and no doubt they may gain some improvement in that time; but the disease can be by
no means cured, and thus much harm is

effected, and they only relapse into a worse state than they were in before. They should be impressed at the outset with the gravity of the complaint, and that without the greatest care and attention to small details they will go from bad to worse, cure then being unattainable, and mere palliation only to be looked for. A patient should therefore be warned at once, and at the outset, that two years at least, and frequently longer, must in all probability be devoted to regaining his health if a cure is to be obtained and not a mere palliation of the active symptoms. Of course this happy result may be obtained in exceptional cases in a much shorter time. It is universally admitted now that an absolute cure can be, and often is effected, though not many years ago it used to be considered an incurable disease. It is impossible, however, to prognosticate with any certainty which cases will recover; for not unfrequently while one makes a good recovery, an apparently equally favourable case will steadily tend to a fatal termination in spite of all treatment.

I must here take the opportunity of returning my most sincere thanks for the great kindness and attention I have personally received at the hands of my professional brethren in the various places I have visited, whether at home or abroad.

I have also to acknowledge my indebtedness to the valuable writings of Dr. Hermann Weber, Dr. Burney Yeo, Dr. Henry Bennet, Dr. Sparks, Dr. Marcet, Dr. Wilson, Dr. Lindsay, Dr. More Madden, etc.

CHAPTER I.

The Ocean as a Health Resort in Phthisis.*

The almost world-wide distribution of phthisis, and the large proportion of deaths caused thereby in nearly every country, a few favoured districts and islands alone being exempt, whilst in many parts of the world it stands in the first place as a cause of death, makes it a subject of special interest to us all. This interest is increased since we find by clinical experience that under careful treatment and favourable circumstances, it is certainly a curable disease. There can be no doubt that climate has a most marked influence for good or evil upon the progress of the disease, and therefore the merits of various places, or so-called health resorts, which have a beneficial influence on the disease, have frequently been

* Reprinted and enlarged from a paper in the *Manchester Medical Chronicle* for August, 1885.

discussed. The ocean, even from ancient times, has always had its advocates as a health resort. Celsus, for instance, one of the most esteemed of ancient medical authors, writes :—"Opus est si vires patiuntur longâ navigatione, coeli mutatione, sic ut densius quam id est ex quo discedit aeger petatur. Ideoque optissime Alexandriam ex Italiâ iter. Si id imbecilletas non sinit, nave tamen sed non longe vectari commodissimum est," *i.e.*, "if the patient's strength allow he must take a long voyage, changing his climate, taking care to seek a denser air than that he leaves, and therefore from Italy to Alexandria is a very suitable change. If the weakness (of the patient) does not allow of that, it is very proper, however, to sail in a ship, but not far."

It is now, however, perhaps more popular than ever, though the popularity of the sailing vessel is perhaps waning in favour of the greater comforts obtainable on the ocean-going steamers. But very numerous are the patients sent off yearly by both sailing vessel and steamer, to try a long sea voyage to Australia, New Zealand, or other distant part of the world, for various complaints, the chief of which, however, is consumption.

Unless a trip be taken in a private yacht, the possibility of taking a voyage in a sailing vessel is now almost confined to the long sea voyage to Australia and New Zealand. It is far otherwise, however, with regard to steamers, for in them a great variety of either long or short voyages may be taken, all in well appointed passenger ships. Perhaps in the way of short voyages, the most satisfactory for the invalid, if only he can refrain from doing too much sight seeing on land at the different points of call, are those which can now be taken in various steam yachts and pleasure steamers to the Mediterranean, to the Canaries, to the Fjords of Norway, and so forth. One great advantage of these trips is that the passengers, and not the cargo or mails, are the first consideration, and thus, for example, such trying and disagreeable necessities as crossing the Tropics are avoided.

Now in this, perhaps, as much as in any

other class of health resort, is it important
to recommend suitable cases. Many and
many are sent out yearly in this manner,
and unattended by friend or relation, only
to be a tie on those around them, and then
eventually to succumb before reaching their
destination ; or if they do survive, are only
in a condition to be drafted into the
hospitals. For instance, Dr. Griffith, of
Melbourne, in a letter to the *British Medical
Journal*, Feb. 9th, 1889, says :—" At the
present moment I have several phthisical
patients under observation in the wards of
the Melbourne Hospital. These have all
arrived recently from London by sailing
ship, after a prolonged endurance of hard-
ship and discomfort, and their condition
was greatly aggravated by the voyage."
Again, he says :—" Last week a gentleman
recently arrived from London consulted me.
He is suffering from tubercular phthisis,
and his condition is quite hopeless ; but he
was advised by a London physician to make
a voyage in a sailing vessel. He was ninety-
four days on the voyage, and very nearly
died during the cold wet weather ; but in

any case he was an unsuitable patient to send abroad for climatic treatment." Medical men too seldom realise what they are advising when they recommend a sea voyage to any but the physically strong; in theory it is all very well, but in practice it is a very different matter. I have seen cases in the third stage of consumption, and that rapidly progressing, sent on board without a friend or even an attendant, to brave all the difficulties, trials, and often real hardships of a long sea voyage. At the same time one must not forget that it is often by the patient's own determination, and against the will of his medical adviser, that he sets out on a voyage, or makes up his mind to go to some much lauded place of which he has read, where he expects to be cured, in however bad a condition he may be.

Though the commissariat on the Ocean Steamers is fairly good, and on good sailing vessels very much improved from what it used to be, nevertheless it is not at all what an invalid should or would have if he were at some health resort on land. It is ad-

mitted that no air is purer, not even that at
the top of a mountain, than that far out at
sea ; but the difference between it and that
of a seaside health resort, well exposed to
sea breezes, must be small, and both are
laden with the saline particles which are
considered so health giving. Any slight
advantage there may be as to the pureness
of the air of the ocean is, I maintain, far
outweighed by the manifest disadvantages
to an invalid at sea, such as the close ill-
ventilated cabins, the draughty saloons, the
weakness and straining caused by sea sickness, the damp sea fogs, the enforced confinement below during bad weather, and the
great trial to an invalid of passing through
the tropics.

A London consultant sent a friend of the
present writer, a short time ago, on a
voyage to Australia, though he had a cavity
forming in his right lung, saying to him,
"Oh! you will be basking in the sunshine
and sleeping out on deck in the fresh air
in a few days," little remembering all the
above mentioned trials he had first to pass
through. And when the wished-for latitude

is reached, with its warm nights, the decks are found to be so damp from the heavy dews that no such thing as the anticipated pleasure of sleeping in the open air is attainable, at all events for an invalid. The above-named gentleman did survive his voyage, but was scarcely strong enough to walk unaided when he landed in Australia ; and of the ten consumptives on board the same vessel, *six*, at least, died amongst strangers in various parts of the Colonies shortly after their arrival.

Has anyone, may I ask, ever heard of such a mortality as that amongst patients sent to any health resort on land, whether at home or abroad, in so short a period? On the other hand, many cases with sufficient strength to withstand the drawbacks which have to be encountered, are greatly benefited by a voyage, and often cured. For instance, H., a professional cricketer, who came under my own notice during a long voyage to Australia, was losing flesh rapidly, and had had hæmoptysis and other signs and symptoms of advancing phthisis. He gained no less than twenty-one pounds during the voyage, and did not have a bad symptom after the first few days at sea. Now it is such cases as this, which so strongly advocate the cause of the ocean as a health resort; but we should find, on examination, that it is those in the early stages of the disease to whom it is most beneficial (a remark, as I have elsewhere mentioned, which is applicable to every health resort), whilst it is simply a fatal remedy to those in advanced stages of the disease. If we trace the course of a sailing ship on such a voyage, does it not stand to reason, that a patient to benefit by it, must be strong enough at starting to withstand the frequent inclemencies of the weather to be met with round our coasts and the other drawbacks already mentioned, and afterwards the depressing effects of the tropics; or again, the cold bad weather so often encountered between the Cape and Australia? If he has not this stamina left in him, he will almost certainly get an exacerbation of the disease which only too frequently ends fatally before the termination of the voyage.

Let us now take for example, the case of a

patient sailing in a well appointed ship in September or October, the most favourable time of the year for starting on a voyage to Australia or New Zealand. Not unfrequently the voyage is commenced by having a delay of a day or two in the Thames or in the Channel, on account of a cold clammy fog, which is most injurious to patients; but if clear, it is generally sharp weather, and the patient finds himself pacing up and down deck to keep himself warm in the cool autumn sea breeze, which frequently necessitates great coats and pea-jackets even for the healthy. As evening comes on, he has to descend into the saloon, only to find such draughts there as would frighten him or his physician if on land! Here he has to remain all the evening with his overcoat and cap on, making the best of it; or if he finds it too unbearable, he tries to take refuge in his private cabin, which he has probably to share with one or two companions, and which he finds very close and quite lacking the fresh air he would obtain in an airy bedroom on shore.

An equinoctial gale is not unusually met

with before getting away from our coasts,
with its concomitant miseries of sea sickness and enforced confinement to the lower
regions of the ship, with their draughts or
want of ventilation, the deck being probably
too wet and slippery for anything but a
struggle to the smoking-room with its
vitiated air.

This uncertain trying weather generally
lasts for the first ten days or even a fortnight, but after this a much more pleasant
time usually sets in during the ship's passage through what is called the calm belt
of Cancer, where the winds are variable and
the temperature much more genial. This
belt of calms and variable winds is generally called the " Horse latitudes " by
sailors, because vessels in old times bound
to the West Indies and laden with horses,
were so frequently delayed in it that the
horses used often to die from want of water.
This pleasant weather lasts also through
the North East trade winds, which begin
to blow steadily at about latitude 30° N.,
but varying with the time of year, and
which carry the ship well into the tropics,

till the Doldrums, or belt of equatorial calms, are reached at a latitude of about 10° N. And here again the patient has to face another most trying period, and another trial of his strength, in the great depression caused by the heat and moisture of this region of the tropics. There are here constant falls of heavy rain, and the atmosphere is most steamy and oppressive. The action of this humid heat results in lessened evaporation from the skin, and diminished exhalation of aqueous vapour from the lungs. A plethoric condition is set up, with a lassitude of the digestive and other functions. The really depressing effect of it may be clearly seen in the healthy, for in the great majority a considerable loss of weight takes place, varying from two to four, or even six pounds, during the period usually spent in the most trying part of the equatorial region. If it is thus felt by the healthy, much more does the patient suffer. If he has been suffering from hæmoptysis or night sweats, the former frequently returns with increased violence, and the latter are rendered much more profuse, and therefore more weakening, while the appetite is almost completely in abeyance. Such real dangers are these, indeed, that not unfrequently advanced cases terminate fatally in this region.

Somewhere a few degrees north of the equator, (about 3° or 4° N. generally), the ship encounters the South-East trade winds, and a most delightful change in the weather takes place, which lasts till a latitude of about 35° S., when a more variable period ensues, till the longitude of the Cape of Good Hope is reached. On entering this part of the voyage the languor of the tropics is thrown off and the patient is braced up; and if tolerably well, regains in this period of about three weeks, the loss of weight he sustained in the preceding fortnight.

The ship now enters the well-known district of the "Roaring-forties," and here trials again await the invalid, for not only is a heavy sea generally met with, but ice is often near at hand, and the cold is so great as to give the majority of patients chills and chilblains, and renders it necessary for the healthy to run about on deck, or take part in athletic exercises to keep warm. The invalid, being unable to join in such pursuits, has to wrap up and keep himself warm as best he can while on deck; but when he has to turn in on account of bad weather or nightfall, no warmth, no fire, is to be obtained, and he has to seek his bunk shivering, with the hope of finding the warmth in bed, which he is unable to obtain elsewhere. This trying weather lasts, more or less continually, till the longitude of the western point of Australia is reached, when it becomes decidedly warmer, and the patient is again able to sit on deck and enjoy the sunshine and his moderate and quiet exercise. This fair weather usually lasts at that time of the year (December) till the ship arrives at her destination, whether it be Melbourne, Sydney, or New Zealand.

Let it not be thought that I have given a prejudiced account of the voyage through personal illness, for on the contrary, I was in very fair health at the time, being able to be on deck in all weathers, and personally, thoroughly enjoyed the voyage, which was taken in what is probably the best appointed passenger ship sailing to the Antipodes, viz., the Sobraon. I could not, however, shut my eyes to the sufferings of others, and should now, in a poorer state of health, dread it exceedingly for myself. It is almost useless to give any meteorological table for such a voyage as has been described, as the temperatures actually observed give no idea whatever of the personal feelings of heat and cold experienced at sea. For instance, the heat in the Doldrums rarely exceeds 85° F., which gives no adequate idea of the most depressing *feeling* of heat experienced there. Again, how inadequately is the bitter cold of the period between the Cape and Australia expressed by a temperature of 40° or 42° F.!

Passenger sailing vessels are now so rapidly becoming superseded by the ocean steamer, that they will before long probably become only a thing of the past. If the voyage is taken in a steamer, instead of a sailing vessel, several advantages are no doubt obtained, but at the same time there are decided disadvantages connected with it.

The saloons of the steamers are more com-
modious and frequently can be warmed in
cold weather; the food is fresher and better,
the tropics are more quickly passed through,
and the danger of being becalmed in the
Doldrums is obviated. On the other hand,
the cabin space is sacrificed for the engines
and large dining-saloon, and four passengers
are not unfrequently crammed into a cabin
of about the same size as would be allowed
for two only, on a sailing vessel; not only
so, there are many cabins which have not
even any access to the outside air at all,
having only a borrowed light. Again, the
transition from cold to warm, and conversely
from warm to cold climates is very much
more rapid, and therefore much more trying
to the invalid than in the case of the sailing
vessel; and thus one of the main characteristics of the ocean climate, viz., its equability, is lost, while the incessant vibration
of the screw is most annoying to many.

Another feature of long sea voyages which
has recently come prominently forward in
the medical journals is the absolute danger,
besides the mere unpleasantness, of a person

being shut up with a phthisical travelling companion in a close, ill-ventilated cabin, for so many hours nightly for weeks together. Dr. Henry Bennet, of Mentone, in the *British Medical Journal* of Feb., 1889, relates a case which came under his own notice, very much to the point and demonstrating the great risk and real danger that may be run. His patient was a captain in the army, aged 27, who had been a model of health and strength all his life, and had scarcely ever known a day's illness. His family history was in every way excellent, with no taint whatever of phthisis. He had been serving in New Zealand and came home in a sailing vessel which took about four months on the voyage, occupying the same cabin with his wife who was in an advanced stage of consumption, and who died three weeks before their arrival in England. Till her death the port-hole was rarely open, and the cabin was consequently most ill-ventilated. He evidently became infected, for within a few weeks after his arrival in England, he developed symptoms of phthisis, and was in an advanced stage of the disease when he consulted Dr. Bennet in the autumn, who soon after heard of his death. As Dr. Bennet well says, "a diseased person has no right to infect the sound public, in endeavouring to save himself," which principle is recognised in compelling isolation in many infectious diseases, such as small-pox; though of course as to the contagiousness of phthisis it does not compare in degree with them, still the danger does exist, as is proved by the above well authenticated case. It seems to me that there should be a largely increased number of single berthed cabins, and that the ship's surgeon should have the power of moving any advanced case of phthisis, and of certain other diseases to a single berthed cabin, both in the interests of the patient himself and of his travelling companion.

Besides the cases of phthisis, of various nervous complaints, of chronic catarrh, of anæmia and debility, of a tendency to scrofulous diseases, etc., for which an ocean voyage is adapted, there is one complaint for which it is sometimes recommended, but which generally ends in a dismal failure,

and that is dipsomania.   Such persons have
nothing to distract their attention and find
very little to interest or amuse them on
board, consequently they quickly fall back
on the 'bar' for excitement.   Even if at last
they are forbidden to be served by order of
the captain or surgeon, there are always
friends or stewards ready to obtain drink
surreptitiously for them.

The following tables of the weights of
passengers taken on a voyage from England
to Melbourne will explain themselves, and
are given for what they are worth; but it
must be kept in mind that the worst patients
often refuse to be weighed at all, whilst
others finding they are losing ground in the
tropics, become disheartened, and will not
again be weighed.

The most notable thing in them, is the
great fall in weight both in the healthy and
the phthisical in the tropics, and the remarkable rebound afterwards in the southern
temperate region.

TABLE.

Weights of passengers taken at intervals of about a fortnight during a voyage to Australia.

The calculations as to relative loss or gain begin with the second time of weighing, and therefore the first weighings are omitted.

SECOND WEIGHINGS, LAT. 28° N.

CLASS I.—Healthy persons, or those suffering from minor complaints.

CLASS II.—Phthisical Patients.

Class I.—Number weighed, 32.

19 gained 64·5 ℔, averaging 3·4 ℔ each.

8 lost 11 ℔, averaging 1·4 ℔ each.

5 neither gained nor lost.

Class II.—Number weighed, 20.

12 gained 28 ℔, averaging 2·33 ℔.

5 lost 9·5 ℔,   ,,   2 ℔ (nearly).

3 neither gained nor lost.

THIRD WEIGHINGS, LAT. 5° N.

Class I.—Number weighed, 36.

5 gained 9 ℔, averaging 1·8 ℔.

27 lost 99 ℔, averaging 3·66 ℔.

4 neither gained nor lost.

Class II.—Number weighed, 15.

3 gained 6·5 ℔, averaging 2·16 ℔.
12 lost 54·5 ℔, averaging 4·54 ℔.

FOURTH WEIGHINGS, LAT. 31° S.

Class I.—Number weighed, 36.

32 gained 111·5 ℔, averaging 3·48 ℔.
3 lost 2·5 ℔, averaging ·83 ℔.
1 neither gained nor lost.

Class II.—Number weighed, 12.

11 gained 54 ℔, averaging 5 ℔ (nearly).
1 lost 4 ℔, averaging 4 ℔.

FIFTH WEIGHINGS, LAT. 39—38' S.

Class I.—Number weighed, 33.

25 gained 54·5 ℔, averaging 2·18 ℔.
5 lost 12·5 ℔, averaging 2·5 ℔.
3 neither gained nor lost.

Class II.—Number weighed, 14.

8 gained 24 ℔, averaging 3 ℔.
3 lost 6 ℔, averaging 2 ℔.
3 neither gained nor lost.

TOTAL VARIATION BETWEEN FIRST AND LAST WEIGHINGS.

Class I.—Number weighed, 38.

29 gained 162·5 ℔, averaging 5·6 ℔.
9 lost 24·5 ℔, averaging 2·73 ℔.
Greatest gain, 13 ℔.

Class II.—Number weighed, 17.

9 gained 78 ℔, averaging 8 66 ℔.
8 lost 16·5 ℔, averaging 2·06 ℔.
Two greatest gains were 20 ℔ and 19 ℔.

CHAPTER II.

A SUMMER IN THE ENGADINE.

SWITZERLAND has now become so familiar
to our countrymen that one might almost
say, who is there that has not at least some
acquaintance with the beauties of that lovely
country, and with the invigorating air of the
playground of Europe? Of all its health-
giving districts, the majority of those who
know it best, would doubtless give the palm
to the Engadine. Here, the very valleys are
between five and six thousand feet above
the sea; so that those who are unable to
climb, and have from physical weakness to
tread the level pathways, are enabled to
breathe in, night and day, the rarified and
invigorating air, causing improved nutrition
and sanguification in the invalid, and stimulating the flagging energies of his system.
For it has been shown that oxygen finds its
way into the blood with increased readiness,
and at the same time the carbonic acid gas

is eliminated from it with a greater degree of facility at a high altitude than at the sea level, and to this fact much of the curative power is due.

The praises of this district have often been loudly sung, and the means of getting there, and other such particulars are amply stated in many a guide book; so these details will be passed over, and we will turn to our more immediate object.

To reach any one of the villages of this elevated region, it must not be forgotten that there is a long and tedious coach drive, most fatiguing to an invalid; and it should, therefore, be broken at one or more of the villages used as stopping places on the chosen route. If a start be made from Coire, the visitor has to be up soon after 4 a.m., and to start in the chilly morning air at about 5 a.m., while the long journey is not accomplished till about 6 p.m., but varying a little with the route and the destination. If the Albula route from Coire is chosen, the journey may be broken at Alvenau or Bergun, or if the Julier route is taken, Tiefenkasten or Mühlen may be the

D

stopping place. Thusis is also a good stopping place, though it is rather too near Coire, but is perhaps most frequently chosen from its having a good, quiet and comfortable hotel. Not only on account of the fatigue should this long drive be broken, but also it is most essential in many cases that the ascent should be performed gradually, so that the heart and lungs may become accustomed by degrees to the rarefaction of the air at those high altitudes.

The long mountain valley of the upper Engadine is divided into two portions at St. Moritz by a natural barrier of elevated ground which runs across the valley; the chief resorts in the upper part of the valley are the Maloja, Sils Maria, Silva Plana, Campfer and St. Moritz, while those most frequented in the lower, are Samaden and Pontresina; the latter is really on a branch valley leading to the Bernina Pass. Although these are all within a few miles of one another, they each possess several distinctive features.

The accommodation at each and all of these places is very good, as also is the

food, though the large and fine Kursaal at
the Maloja has the reputation of carrying off
the palm in these respects, its spacious and
well ventilated reception rooms being its
special recommendation. Granting the
many favourable things that have been said
of this district, there are certainly some
drawbacks connected with it, which an
invalid must take into consideration: firstly,
the almost constant high wind sweeping up
and down the valley; secondly, the quantities of *dust* in the roads which is blown
about in clouds by this wind; thirdly, the
sudden and great changes of temperature
which occasionally take place; and fourthly,
the overcrowding of the hotels during the
height of the season, and consequently the
frequent impossibility of obtaining good
rooms suitable for an invalid. As regards
the first of these points, the Maloja, Campfer, and St. Moritz are the chief sufferers,
being exposed to the full current of air
which blows along the valley, while Sils
Maria and Pontresina are decidedly more
sheltered. In fact the difference in the
amount of wind at St. Moritz and Pon-

tresina on the same day is frequently astonishing.

It is said that the latter is exposed to cold draughts of air at times, coming down the valley from the Roseg glacier, but I cannot say I felt it when there. The Maloja hotel being placed immediately on the exposed summit of the Maloja Pass, as it rises from the warm plains of Italy, perhaps gets the wind as badly as any place, though the anemometer there seemed ingeniously placed so as to show as little wind as possible! A diligence driver was asked if he generally found it windy on that road, and his answer was, "that he had driven the coach every day for between twenty and thirty years, and he had never yet found it anything but windy!" In fine weather the local valley wind generally rises between nine and ten in the morning and blows hard all day till about six in the evening, when it sub-sides. This is most aggravating for those who are susceptible to winds, for few invalids are able to go out before breakfast, and most are not allowed to be out after sunset.

Secondly, as to dust; perhaps in this

respect Campfer is the worst, for as both the hotels are situated immediately on the high road, they are often enveloped in clouds of dust, and the grass in the fields is frequently white with it. This quantity of dust is not only unpleasant, but when carried about in the air is irritating to the lungs.

Thirdly, as to changes of temperature; these are often sudden and decided, therefore plenty of warm clothing should be taken, as it is not at all unfrequently the case for there to be two or three falls of snow even in the warmest month—that of August. It seldom lies in the valleys for more than a few hours, but it is generally accompanied by a cold N.E. wind, and is a great and sudden change to an invalid, who has been sitting out daily and basking in the hot sunshine usually experienced in fine weather. Occasionally a bad season or a few weeks of really bad weather is experienced in these high valleys with almost constant rain, mists, snow showers and cold, rendering the climate unfit for delicate invalids. They should therefore endeavour to ascertain before leaving their lower and warmer quarters that the weather is fairly good and settled.

Fourthly, as to accommodation ; a south or sunny bedroom should be chosen ; a little sunshine in cold or gloomy weather makes a wonderful difference in the room, so a south one should not be overlooked or neglected even in summer. In order, therefore, to get a choice of rooms, it is better to go early in the season, otherwise an invalid may find himself packed away in some dark and dreary little room, which is anything but conducive to health. In the height of the season it is often almost impossible to obtain any accommodation at all, even though the hotels have so vastly increased their resources of late years, and new arrivals may have to put up with a shake-down in the billiard room or elsewhere for some days. This applies perhaps more especially to Pontresina.

Summing up the special aspects of these various summer resorts in this extensive valley ; we have standing at the head of the valley the magnificent Kursaal of the

Maloja, situated at the summit of the pass, at an elevation of 5,688 feet, well known in connection with Dr. Tucker Wise's writings on the "Alpine Winter." Its excellent management, its admirable system of ventilation, its numerous and spacious reception rooms, its fine airy corridors and many other advantages are well known. Nevertheless, its position is unfortunately chosen, being greatly exposed to winds, as before stated, and also being placed too near, and too much on the same level, as the Lake. The swampy, damp and boggy ground at the end of the Lake of Sils, which itself is only two or three hundred yards from the hotel, approaches it far too closely, for unhealthy emanations arise from it; besides which there is scarcely sufficient fall for the drainage when the lake is full, thus causing backward pressure up the sewers. They are, however, well trapped, so that no sewer gas can enter the building.

Sils Maria, on the southern side of the valley (5,880 feet) is very quiet, and is well protected from the "Thal" or valley wind. Here, one is removed from the stir and bustle of St. Moritz and Pontresina, while the hotels are comfortable and some distance from the dusty high road.

Campfer, still further down the valley, is capitally situated, at an elevation of 5,950 feet, on the north side of the valley, and well removed above the damp fields by the river side. Both hotels are good and comfortable, but much exposed to the valley wind, and to the dust from the high roads. This place is most conveniently situated for those who wish to take the waters at St. Moritz, and yet wish to avoid the fashion and bustle of that place, and to rusticate after the fatigues of a London season or the drudgery of a city office. The walk through the pine woods of a mile and a half to and from the Trinkhalle at St. Moritz Bad is very enjoyable, and much more pleasant than the steep and dusty high-road to the Kulm.

In the valley below St. Moritz, are Samaden and Pontresina. The former at an elevation of 5,700 feet and three miles below St. Moritz, is much less interesting and pretty than the other villages; but it forms a useful " overflow " for visitors who cannot get the accommodation they require at Pontresina or at St. Moritz, and who have to wait there and "bide their time."

Pontresina situated at the same elevation as Campfer, *i.e.*, 5,950 feet is, with the English, the most popular of the Engadine resorts. It is also about three miles from St. Moritz, but situated in a branch valley, that leading to the Bernina Pass. It is a splendid centre for mountain excursions, and is therefore very much given up to the tourist during the summer months. It is said to suffer from the cold winds off the Roseg Glacier to which it lies exposed; but however this may be, for we have not noticed it ourselves, it is most certainly far less exposed to the daily strong valley wind, so much felt in the main valley of the Engadine.

Tourists too often consider Pontresina, and some other such places, essentially their happy hunting grounds, and seem to think that no delicate person has any right to intrude on these their own peculiar domains, which often renders these places trying to invalids. Dr Sparks thus speaks on this point :* " In summer the tourist is supreme, whether he invades your would-be solitude by parties of two or three, or in Cook-led multitudes of fifty or sixty . . . . . . He rises at 3 a.m., and sometimes at 2 a.m., and the sound of his bath wakes you through the thin pine-wood wall. The night is his, and, with calm indifference to the surrounding sleepers, he stamps with his heavy feet and whistles in the corridors. All this, and much more, without the least exaggeration, the tourist, and most of all the British tourist, does to annoy his fellow-men and demonstrate his own selfishness. In so doing he renders some of the best parts of Switzerland unfit for the abode of delicate people."

St. Moritz is the central and most fashionable of the Engadine resorts, and is especially patronised by Germans and foreigners generally, on account of its baths and mineral chalybeate waters.

Many delicate persons are sent there to take the waters ; while many others take them, although there may not be much the

* *The Riviera*, Edward Sparks.

matter with their health; for a German
would never consider that he could obtain
any good from a holiday and change of air,
unless he partook of the waters and used the
baths regularly, at some one of these numerous springs in his own or in a neighbouring
country! The village of St. Moritz Dorf is
situated on the side of the mountain, about
300 feet above the valley where the
Kurhaus and springs are. It is much exposed to winds, and the high road forms a
rather long and dusty climb for those who
have to go down daily for the waters, though
there are plenty of conveyances for those
who wish for them.

St. Moritz Bad has two chalybeate
springs, the Alte Quelle and the Paracelsus;
the latter contains the larger proportion of
carbonate of iron and is the one usually
drunk, the water from the other being used
chiefly for the baths. The Paracelsus water,
even, does not contain half as much iron as
the Tunbridge Wells water, but is strongly
charged with carbonic acid gas, and is
quite pleasant and refreshing to drink,
notwithstanding the chalybeate taste, which

is by no means strong. These springs were known to the ancient Romans, but they have only been used by modern Europe for the last two centuries. To take a series of 20 to 25 baths is considered an essential part of the cure to be obtained there, at all events by foreigners; but the truth of this we greatly doubt. The water is heated by jets of steam being forced into it, till it is raised to a temperature of 90° to 95° F. The patient has to remain in the bath from 20 minutes to half an hour; the bath being covered over by a wooden lid with a hole in it for the head, which alone remains visible. In some few cases the stimulating effects of the carbonic acid in the water may be of some value, while the mere immersion in the water is soothing to others. But as Dr. Burney Yeo   in his "Health Resorts" "If the good these baths do be in many cases problematical, the *harm* they occasion in some instances is by no means doubtful."

I have, myself, known debilitated ladies who have been ostensibly sent up to the Engadine for its bracing and stimulating air, come back from the baths, day after day, in a semi-exhausted condition, declaring "they did not really know whether they would be able to last out the course, for there were yet ten or twelve (whatever it might be) more to take!" Still they would persevere with the baths because they had been ordered to take them, though they felt and acknowledged their debilitating influence. Again, there are many cases where the sudden change of temperature and atmosphere from the hot and steamy air of the bath-rooms, laden with moisture, to the keen air outside, cannot but be harmful, more especially when the skin is relaxed and sodden with long immersion in hot water. If the Swiss physicians exercised a little more discretion, and allowed those persons who feel fatigued and exhausted after the baths, instead of invigorated, to leave them off before the "course" was finished, confining them to merely drinking the waters, and thus permitting them to be braced up by the invigorating air of the mountains, then doubtless better results, even than at present, might accrue.

In fact what is wanted here, as is often the case elsewhere, is more elasticity of treatment ; for the human constitution defies a rule-of-thumb treatment.   I feel sure that the chief therapeutic agent at work there, is the pure and bracing mountain air, while the baths and water-drinking are only a useful adjunct in certain cases.

The hotels do not open throughout the Engadine till July 1st, except in the case of those kept open during the winter ; while the real season does not begin till the middle of the month, and only lasts till the middle of September.

Though I shall enter more fully upon the therapeutic influence of altitude when speaking of Davos Platz, still here I may shortly consider what cases are likely to benefit by a summer residence in the Engadine, for on this point there have been many misconceptions, and I may also shortly state in what cases a residence there, and the partaking of the waters of St. Moritz, should be avoided.

Firstly.—In anæmia and chlorosis.

These cases are generally wonderfully

benefited by a stay there, and the mild chalybeate water is a most useful adjunct, though as the amount of iron is very small, it is sometimes useful to supplement it by iron in other forms.

Secondly.—A residence in the Engadine is often most valuable in convalescence from severe illnesses, such as typhoid fever, diphtheria, and other debilitating diseases.

Thirdly.—The beneficial results of a holiday spent in the invigorating air of St. Moritz or Pontresina to the jaded and overworked, are well known, as well as in cases of general weakness from constitutional causes.

The pale and careworn features of the professional or business man, the languid and listless step of the debilitated, the capricious and fanciful appetite of the dyspeptic, soon give place to the well-tanned face, the springy elastic tread, and the hearty appetite of the healthy tourist or mountaineer. The great risk in these cases is, that they should exhaust their newly found vigour, instead of putting by a reserve of energy and harbouring their strength for

future use. Early cases of phthisis should
be particularly warned against this risk ; for
such patients are often deceived as to the
measure of their improvement, and imagine
that with cessation of fever, and of night
sweats, with improved appetite and returning energy, they have practically recovered,
only to be bitterly undeceived by a serious
relapse or hæmorrhage from endeavouring
to do what they see the healthy around them
doing, and to undertake similar excursions.
This lesson has been deeply impressed upon
myself by bitter personal experience.

Dr. Henry Bennet thus speaks on this
point :—" Those who do the best are those
who accept their position cheerfully, who
secede entirely from the valid part of the
population, from their amusements and oc-
cupations, and are content to lead a quiet,
contemplative existence. Happy are they
if they can find pleasure in books, music,
sketching, and the study of nature ; if they
can be satisfied to spend their days in the
vicinity of the house in which they live, and
to sit or lie for hours basking in the sun,
like an invalided lizard on the wall, follow-

ing implicitly the rules laid down for their guidance."

As simple altitude without the aid of the intense cold of an Alpine winter, which so many find too trying for them, has been amply demonstrated to be one of the chief prophylactic and curative agents in this most dangerous, but still curable disease of phthisis, more advantage should be taken of the summer season in these regions, it seems to me, than is usually done by patients. Instead of hurrying home from their warm winter quarters, and often undoing much of the good they have obtained by wintering abroad, they should then ascend to these high altitude stations for the summer. They would then obtain most of the advantages said to be obtained by wintering in Alpine regions, without running the great risk there no doubt is for many invalids from the intense cold of the winter.

The air, certainly, during the summer months, is not so dry (*i.e.*, the absolute humidity is greater) as during the intense cold of winter, for the air is then incapable

E

of holding so much moisture in suspense, but still the dryness at that elevation is considerable. There are also more impurities and dust in the air than when the ground is covered with snow, but with judicious selection of residence, this evil may be reduced to a minimum ; while on the other hand, the evil of living for so many hours a day in over-heated rooms is avoided.

Persons with heart or kidney disease, should as a rule not go to these high elevations even in the summer ; nor indeed should those with brain affections, such as epilepsy, or those who have a tendency to apoplexy.

The widely spread idea which used to prevail, that high altitudes caused hæmoptysis in cases of phthisis, has been amply disproved by practical experience ; but where there is a tendency to it, the waters of St. Moritz should be avoided.

DAVOS PLATZ.—WINTER.

CHAPTER III.

A Winter at Davos.

This favourite winter resort is so well known at the present day, both from the ample literature regarding it, and from the many who have paid it a longer or shorter visit, either on account of health or pleasure, that it requires no detailed description of mine. Davos Platz has its "devoted friends and its bitter enemies," but it is by far the most popular of the Alpine winter resorts, and indeed, it has become so much so, that an outcry has been raised lest it should lose some of its peculiar aptitude for invalids :— firstly, by the increasing amount of smoke created, which in the still atmosphere of winter in this narrow valley, frequently hangs like a cloud over the village, vitiating the atmosphere, and thus doing away with one of its chief advantages and attractions, namely, the absence of all dust and irritating particles in the air ; and secondly, by

the aggregating together of a large number
of persons and houses, which has been fully
proved to be one of the most fruitful causes
of phthisis, and to the absence of which in
mountainous regions and amongst the
nomadic tribes of the world, much of the
immunity of the inhabitants is due.

The canalisation of the Landwasser, the
small river flowing through the valley, is a
very great improvement, and has greatly
diminished the mists which used to rise
from the river and from the damp and peaty
meadows along its banks on either side.
These mists are not yet, however, entirely ·
prevented as has been asserted; for I have
frequently seen them in the early morning,
lying over the river and low meadows, before the sun had risen sufficiently to disperse
them; but they do not, as a rule, rise so
high as to envelop any of the English
hotels, which are all situated on higher
ground on the north side of the valley. In
this respect the elevated position of St.
Moritz Kulm, above the valley and lake, is
an advantage it possesses over Davos.

The main drainage scheme, by which the

whole drainage of the valley is carried down
below the village, before it is permitted to
enter the river, is a great improvement to
the sanitary condition of the locality. It
would, however, be a great advantage if the
authorities could do something to prevent
the atrocious smells that occasionally come
from the cowsheds in the meadows below
the hotels, where the manure is allowed to
collect for too long a time before being removed.

The water supply is excellent, being
brought down in pipes from reservoirs on
the Fluela Pass. The sanitary, heating and
ventilating arrangements of the hotels are
excellent, at least in comparison with the
majority of continental hotels, and there is
much more to praise than to find fault with ;
though there may be minor things which
might be altered with advantage.

The adverse criticisms which one hears
so freely expressed in those resorts, *where
they do not require stove heat*, as to the un-
healthiness of living nineteen or twenty
hours or more out of the twenty-four, in
overheated and unventilated rooms, are, to

a certain extent, unjust; though thorough
ventilation is most difficult in such a cold
climate, without causing dangerous draughts,
where the temperature is so different outside
from what it is inside the house. The
public rooms certainly tend to get over-
heated, and I have frequently seen the
thermometer in the "salon," in the evenings,
standing at 76° or 78° F., though the physicians' rule is that the sitting rooms should
not be kept over 60° F., nor the bed-rooms
over 55°, and this, with the ventilator, *i.e.*,
the upper part of the window which falls
inwards, so as to shoot the incoming air up
towards the ceiling, kept constantly open.
The electric light has been introduced with
much advantage into the Buol hotel, thus
doing away with the smelly paraffin lamp
and its vitiating action on the air.

The contemplated railway from Ragatz
to Davos, already opened as far as Klosters,
has been looked forward to with various feelings; with dire apprehension by some, but
with favour by others. Inherently, it cannot
but increase the growing cloud of smoke
which has already been a cause of complaint,

and in fact has truly become a " burning "
question there. Also through rendering coal
cheaper, it will make it more generally used,
instead of the much less smoke-producing
wood or charcoal now generally burnt.

On the other hand, there are compensating
advantages ; the chief of which to the invalid will be the avoidance of the long,
tedious, and sometimes, to him, dangerous
coach drive to and from Coire. Fresh pro-
visions, such as vegetables and fish, will
also be more readily obtained.

With reference to the winter climate of
Davos, though there has been much said as
to the hot sunshine, the cloudlessness and
the intense blueness of the sky, the dry and
still atmosphere, when once the *true* winter
weather has set in, yet little has been said
of the dreadful period generally preceding
it, when the weather for a month, or frequently six weeks, is as bad and as trying,
save for the fogs, as anything to be met
with in England, and often with even less
sunshine than in our more favoured southern
resorts, such as Ventnor or Eastbourne.
Nor do we often hear of the disastrous

effects of a bad winter there, when there is
a continuance of such weather as generally
precedes the snowfall, and the "glorious
winter weather" only occurs for a week or
two at a time, with intervening longer
periods of absence of sun, and the only too
frequent presence of heavy snowstorms and
bitterly cold winds. At these times it would
be quite unsafe for invalids to venture out
of doors, and even healthy individuals do
not go out if they can avoid it; or if they
do, they return with blue noses and pinched
up features! Mr. J. A. Symonds has stated
in an article in the "Fortnightly Review,"
that there is not a single day (or was not
during the season he wrote) on which he
could not venture out of doors; and that
more liberties can be taken in the air of
Davos than anywhere else. Now my experience has been precisely the reverse, and
nowhere have I had to take so many precautions, or be so careful, as at Davos.
That greater liberties can be taken by invalids in that climate than might have been
expected, is true enough; and one is as-
tonished to see on what bad days some

delicate people do venture out without being
the worse for it. Probably the average experience lies between the two extremes; but
it is a mistake, and even wrong, to encourage
people to imagine they are to enjoy entire
immunity from chills in a climate which is
admittedly prone to cause acute inflam-
mations, such as pleurisy and congestion of
the lungs.

Again, it is often said, " that the cold is
scarcely felt, and the chilly feelings of an
English winter are not known." This may
possibly be true enough for the few with
whom it thoroughly agrees; but it is an
exaggeration in the case of the majority of
visitors, whether invalids or not. As to
myself, I suffered very much more from the
cold there than in England; as also did
those relations of mine, who were with me,
and who were in good health. No doubt it
is very warm just in the direct rays of the
sun, but one cannot be in the sunshine
always, even on sunny days, while there are
many days when there is no sunshine at all
to be in. On sunny days the contrast between the sun and shade temperatures is

enormous, often over 100° F.,* and is therefore most trying.

Frequently extraordinary statements are
made as to the weather at Davos, which
often profess to be based on reliable statistics. If so, the years must have been
picked out as affording exceptionally good
results. For instance, I have a book before
me (Dr. Lindsay on the "Climatic Treatment of Consumption") which gives a table
of the average number of cloudy days for
the respective winter months for an average
of three years ; the years are not specified,
so I cannot verify them, but in the table the
average of cloudy days for the months of
October, December and January is given as
"less than one each." This is to me a
most misleading statement. The book was
published in 1887, so I do not know whether
the table included December, 1886, in which
there were only 42¾ hours of sunshine
throughout the month, with fifteen completely overcast, besides seven cloudy days,
sufficient in that one year to make the
average given for *fifteen* years at least, if not
for *twenty-two* !! Even adding the average

* Blackened bulb *in vacuo.*

number of " wet and snowy days," which I
presume were also cloudy, though their not
being included under that category renders
the table very misleading, which are given
as only two for October, one for December,
and two for January; and including also the
number of days in which "some rain or
snow fell," even then I cannot reconcile the
table with the facts of the case. For again,
in the same month rain or snow fell on
twenty-two days, while the average given is
six, so again that one month would nearly
make up the average stated for four years.

Again, Professor Charteris in his work on
" Health Resorts " makes the astonishing
statement :—" During the season of 1881-82
there was at Davos a clear unclouded sky
from the beginning of November to the end
of March." Unfortunately I cannot obtain
the statistics of the weather for that year,
but the correctness of the statement may be
gathered from the fact that in the exceptionally fine season of 1879-80, " perhaps one of
the most perfect ever known in the Alps "
(Yeo) rain or snow fell on thirty-six days between November and March !

Let us examine the season of 1886-1887, the winter of which was an averagely good one; January and February being perhaps better, and December rather worse than the average;—the season I spent there. The following tables are taken from the official monthly record.

TABLE I.

		Oct.	Nov.	Dec.	Jan.	Feb.	Mar.
Barometer.	Highest .	25·26	25·15	24·91	25·32	25·35	25·27
	Average .	24·80	24·84	24·62	24·83	24·99	24·79
	Lowest .	24·18	24·46	24·09	24·06	24·69	24·23
Temp.	Maximum . .	68·2	52·3	44·1	32·9	40·5	48·7
	Average . . .	42·1	30·2	22·1	15·1	17·7	26·6
	Minimum. . .	27·5	4·1	—4·2	—6·	—4·9	—4·9
Sunshine, hours. . . .		140	84	42¾	136¾	147¼	135½
Rainfall, millimetres .		50·2	52·4	87·3	6·6	4·9	43·1
Humidity	Relative .	78 p.c.	84	87·3	87·97	81·55	80·32
	Absolute in mm. of Mercury.	5·18	3·67	2·78	2·09	2·11	2·96
							Total
Sky. Number of days.	Cloudless .	11	10	2	23	18	9=73
	Clear. . . .	10	3	7	3	4	4=31
	Cloudy. . .	4	9	7	2	1	9=32
	Overcast . .	6	8	15	3	5	9=46
	Rain or snow. . .	10	11	22	2	4	15=64

From this table it will be seen that during the winter season October, 1886, to March, 1887, the mean pressure of the barometer was 24·82 ; the mean temperature was

24·6° F., and that of the months December, January and February, 18·2°; the mean lowest temperature for any month being 15° for January, and the lowest temperature recorded —6° F.

The average number of hours of sunshine was 114·3, while in December there were only 42¾°; the rainfall amounted to 244·5 mm., or nearly ten inches of rain; snow falling on fifty-five days, and rain on nine, or a total of sixty-four days on which rain or snow fell. The mean relative humidity was 83·1, being the mean of three daily observations taken at 7 a.m., 1 p.m., and 9 p.m.; there were seventy calm days, fifty-seven breezy, and fifty-five windy and stormy. The sky was cloudless on seventy-three days; clear, but not cloudless on thirty-one days; cloudy on thirty-two, and completely overcast on forty-six; or a total of one hundred and four clear or sunny days, and seventy-eight more or less densely cloudy.

TABLE II.

If Table I. be now extended so as to include the seasons of 1886-7, 1887-8,

1888-89, we find the following aver-
ages :—

	1886-7.	1887-8.	1888-9.	MEAN FOR 3 YEARS.
Mean Temperature . . .	25·6	24·8	27·5	25·7° F.
Mean Temperature of Dec., Jan. and Feb. .	18·2	20·0	23·0	20·4° F.
Average hours of sunshine.	114·3	101·0	124·0*	113·0
Rainfall. . . . . . . mm.	244·5	408·3	273·0	308·6 or 12·4 inches.
Days of rain or snow . .	64	75	48	62·3
Mean relative humidity.	83 p.c.	84·	78··	81·7
Sky. Very clear.	73	64	76	71·0
Clear but not cloudless	31	35	43	36·3
Cloudy	32	28	20	26·6
Completely overcast.	46	56	43	48·3

TABLE III.

Showing the average number of clear and
cloudy days for the several winter months
of the three years 1886-1889.

	OCT.	NOV.	DEC.	JAN.	FEB.	MARCH.
Very clear . .	14·3	9·7	10·0	19·3	10·0	7·7
Clear	6·3	4·7	6·7	4·3	5·7	8·7
Cloudy	4·0	7·3	3·3	3·0	3·3	6·3
Overcast . . .	6·3	9·3	11·0	4·3	9·3	8·3

* For three months only; the statistics for the last
three months of this season are extracted from the
very good reports issued by the proprietors of the
Belvedere Hotel.

Thus it will be seen that October had on an average, 10 cloudy days, November 16, December 14, January 7, February 12, and March 14 ; a very good winter record but scarcely coinciding with the table referred to before as given by Dr. Lindsay.

As every one knows, Davos and the other Alpine resorts are visited during the winter chiefly by phthisical patients, and it is that large class of invalids which has been chiefly benefited by a winter's residence in those high altitudes, and in the intensely cold atmosphere experienced there. The idea of sending such patients to such a climate would have appeared mere madness to the last generation, and yet now the danger is of pressing it too far, and of sending phthisical patients there without due care, and without first ascertaining whether they are suitable cases for such rigorous treatment. In fact it has now become the fashion to send those who have any weakness of the chest there, just as it was the fashion thirty or forty years ago to indiscriminately order patients to Torquay or to Madeira.

The great revolution that has been wrought during the last generation in the treatment of phthisis, and I may add in the percentage of cures, has been brought about by the recognition of the fact on the one hand, that it is essentially a disease of debility and mal-nutrition, whether acquired or inherited, often induced, and always intensified, by living in a vitiated or impure atmosphere and in unhygienic surroundings of any kind; while on the other hand, the main factor in its cure is free ventilation in the house, and as far as possible, living an *open-air life*, which improves nutrition and counteracts the morbid tendency of the blood and tissues.

This revolution in treatment has been since further promoted, and the above view strengthened, firstly, by the actual results obtained by treatment at high altitudes, and secondly, by the comparatively recent discovery of Koch's tubercular bacillus. It is not that these discoveries have revolutionized the treatment of phthisis, as has been urged, for it had become generally recognised that the old plan of treatment, by

keeping the patient in a close hot room with
no ventilation lest he should catch cold, and
on low diet lest the fever should be increased,
was a complete mistake. So it came to be
acknowledged, that free ventilation and improved general nutrition were the essential
factors, not only in the cure, but in the
prophylactic warding off of this fell disease.
The Alpine treatment has only been a
further development of this theory, as
affording to some constitutions a more
powerful antidote to their mal-nutrition.
Again, no medicinal agent, whether taken
internally or locally applied by inhalation or
other means, has been proved to have any
specific power over the bacilli in diminishing
their numbers, and that this result, if effected,
is only accomplished through the improved
resisting power of the tissues brought about
by a better nutrition.

The discovery of the tubercular bacillus—
apart from its great value as a means of
diagnosis—has only proved more fully that
it is the weakened tissues which form a congenial nidus for the development of the
disease; and that it is only by these hygienic

means their dire effects may be counter-
acted. This result, naturally, is most easily
effected in the first stage of the disease,
where there is only some consolidation, or
where there has been hæmoptysis without
much local or constitutional manifestation
of the disease to undermine the patient's
physical strength and general health; and
therefore it is, that if one consults a mono-
graph, whether it be on Davos, or on the
Riviera, on Madeira, or on the value of sea
voyages, one always finds it stated "that
the greatest amount of good may be expected in the early stages of the disease."
This may, certainly, therefore be said of all
climates, still the Alpine winter climate
seems more frequently capable than any
other, of checking that steady and irresistible
onward progress of the disease, which in so
many cases tends rapidly to a fatal termination in spite of all treatment. It must, however, be remembered that there is no dog-
matic rule to go by, and not unfrequently
cases that seem going only from bad to
worse in the cold climate of Davos, take a
good turn and begin to improve as soon as

they go to a locality with a warmer and
more congenial temperature.

"There frequently seems," as Dr. Burney
Yeo says, "some special relation between
the individual to be cured and the particular
climate that will suit him, and frequently it
is only by actual trial that such a relation
can be discovered." This raises the important point which I think is not sufficiently
acted upon, that if the Alpine climate does
not manifestly suit a patient, it is far better
for him to leave at once for a lower altitude
and a warmer temperature, rather than to
try and brave it out, as he is frequently en-
couraged to do, with the hope of its ulti-
mately suiting him. As a rule it is quickly
manifest whether the climate does or does
not suit a patient; and if it does not, no
scruple should be felt in sending him away.
The idea too prevalent there, and which is
often openly expressed is, that the Riviera,
Madeira and other such milder resorts are
well enough to go to, when all hope of a
cure or arrest of the disease has to be aban-
doned, but that if the patient has done badly
at Davos, it seems to be held that the hope

of improvement elsewhere must be given up. Many patients, unfortunately, also become infected with this erroneous notion, probably from the wonderful improvement they see around them in favourable cases, and, becoming disheartened at their own non-success, give up hope and the endeavour to find a climate elsewhere which may suit them better.

Now if we examine the characteristics of this Alpine climate, and the curative agencies at work, we find there :—

(1). Great altitude with its attendant low barometrical pressure, and rarefaction of the air.

(2). Great absolute dryness of the air, though not a low rainfall.

(3). Very low temperature of the air, with great sunheat from the increased Diathermancy of the atmosphere.

(4). Great purity of the air, from the absence of both organic and inorganic particles during the period that the ground is covered with snow, *i.e.*, a remarkable aseptic condition of the air, as Hermann Weber terms it.

(5). A rocky and dry subsoil.

(6). A scanty and sparse population.

Of these characteristics there is not one to which alone we can attribute any specific curative power; it is only in the combination of these several factors that the efficacy of Alpine climates, in suitable cases, is due. Yet even with the combination of all these favourable conditions, it not only fails in many cases, but does not even provide any complete immunity from phthisis to the healthy; for in several cases it has been proved that this disease has originated at Davos.

Though there is no one character, unless it be great purity of air, common to all districts which enjoy an absolute or relative immunity from phthisis, yet the most prominent and general characteristics of such districts are :—

(*a*). Elevation and the consequent rarefaction of the air.

(*b*). Purity of the atmosphere.

(*c*). Dryness of the air.

(*d*). A scanty population.

As will be seen above, the Alpine districts

possess all these characteristics during the winter months; we may now enquire more fully into them.

(1). *The altitude.*—The mean barometrical pressure at Davos is only about 24·80. The effects of lessened barometrical pressure on the body at such moderate heights as that of Davos, 5,125 feet, are not easily separated from the effects of temperature and humidity, which are so much influenced by elevation, directly and indirectly. Respirations are increased both in number (at first) and in depth, to supply the amount of oxygen required by the body; for there is a lessening amount of oxygen in a given measure of air as elevation increases; though it is said that up to a height of 10,000 feet, there is an excess of oxygen in the air over the amount that the blood can absorb from it when respired. The number of respirations, however, is rarely permanently increased (according to Dr. Ruedi, in only 5 per cent. of cases), for as a rule after acclimatisation, the respirations return to their normal number or are even lessened in number; but to compensate for this their

depth is increased; thus bringing the respiratory muscles into more active play, and
thus, as has been amply proved by Dr. C.
T. Williams and others, the chest becomes
expanded and shows an increased measure-
ment of even two to three inches. There is
also an increased flow of blood to the skin,
thus improving its nutrition and strengthen-
ing it against chills. The rapid healing of
cuts and wounds of the skin has often been
noticed. Marcet has proved that under
diminished pressure the oxygen finds its way
into the blood with increased readiness, and
the carbonic acid also passes out of it with
a greater degree of facility. He also found
that the actual amount of carbonic acid
expired at high elevations was increased.
There is, therefore, improved sanguification,
and the general nutrition is promoted.

The practical efficacy of altitude in consumption, was proved long before the Alpine
winter cure was advocated or came into
fashion. For a couple of centuries the
inhabitants of Mexico and of South America,
have known and taken advantage of its
beneficent effects, and it has been their cus-

tom for this long period, to go to high ground
in the plains of Mexico, or to the high valleys
amongst the peaks of the Andes.   In these
regions altitude is unaccompanied by cold,
there being great equability of temperature,
and but little difference between summer
and winter ; the mean annual temperature of
Santa Fé de Bagota at an altitude of 9000
feet being given as 57° F., while the temperature of Quito (9352 feet) is 59° F. in January,
and 60·5° in June !   These places of long
proved efficacy in the treatment of consumption, possess a climate contrasting in
many respects with that of the European
Alpine resorts, though both possess high
altitude and rarefaction of the air.   This
shows, therefore, that the intense cold of
the Alpine winter is not such an important
factor in the cure of the disease as is sometimes thought to be the case.   These South
American resorts, however, are lacking in
two great desiderata for Europeans, namely,
accessibility and good accommodation.

Though the importance of altitude is thus
seen to be very great, it is not a *sine quâ
non* in the cure of phthisis ; for we find

immunity from it on the Tartar Steppes,
which are below the sea-level, and the
curative power of sea air is well known.

(2). *The humidity.*—The annual rainfall,
the number of days on which the rain falls,
and the relative humidity at Davos are all
high, being about 43 inches, 157 days and
83 per cent. respectively; but, on the contrary, the *absolute* humidity of the air is very
low.

Now, the relative humidity of the air
indicates the actual percentage of moisture
in the air relatively to the largest amount it
could possibly contain at the temperature at
which it has been calculated, without de-
positing moisture in the shape of fog or
rain. So in meteorology, the results obtained by estimating the relative humidity
are of great value. It is also of importance,
physiologically speaking; for of course a
relatively dry air at any given temperature
can absorb more moisture than damp air of
the same temperature, though this aspect
has a tendency to be ignored by the advocates of cold dry climates, with a high relative, but with a low absolute humidity.

The influence of the relative humidity has as great an effect on the action cf the skin as it has on that of the lungs ; for the drier an atmosphere (relatively) may be, the greater is the evaporation from the skin as well as from the lungs.

The absolute humidity, however, is the absolute quantity of aqueous vapour which is suspended in a given volume of air. The lower the temperature of the air, the less must be the absolute humidity, whatever the relative humidity may be, for the former varies directly with the temperature. Thus, though the relative humidity of Davos is much higher than that of Madeira, the absolute humidity is far less ; and it is abso- lutely as well as physiologically drier, for the air can absorb far more moisture from the lungs, because the temperature at the former place is so much lower than at the latter, while the body temperature is the same in both.

The air in passing through the lungs is always raised to a temperature approaching that of the body, whatever may have been its temperature when inhaled. The percent-

ages of relative humidity when applied for
physiological comparisons, should therefore
always be reduced to a uniform temperature. " Thus the relative humidity of Davos
is 83·8, and that of Madeira only 69·7, but if
these are reduced to the temperature of the
body, Davos has only 7·1 per cent., and
Madeira 22·8 per cent." (Dr. Reimer).
The absolute humidity is therefore the
best standard to take with respect to the
influence of the air of a climate on the
pulmonary respiration, for the facts and
figures so obtained remain invariable, and
are always at once available for comparison.
Though "moisture *per se* does not occasion
an increase in phthisis " (H. Weber), yet as
a rule localities possessing an immunity
from phthisis, are characterised by considerable dryness of the air, *e.g.*, high altitudes and
dry inland plains. To this, however, there
is a great exception, which proves that
dampness of the air is not necessarily
accompanied by an increase of phthisis, and
that is, the curative power of sea air and the
immunity from phthisis enjoyed by certain
sea-girt islands, such as the Faröe Islands,

as well as as the rarity of the disease among
our seafaring population generally.

(3). *The temperature.*—The low winter
temperature experienced in the Alpine
resorts, has a very decided influence on the
body, causing a greatly increased loss of
heat, both through the lungs and skin.

In healthy persons this stimulates tissue-
change throughout the body, causing improvement of appetite and greater muscular
and nervous vigour. But it must be remembered that these results do not by any
means apply to the old, to the weakly, and
to many who are organically unsound. In
them, cold instead of stimulating, only de-
presses the vital functions. Again, "dry air
combined with a very low temperature irri-
tates the respiratory organs and produces in
them a tendency to inflammatory affections,
particularly to pneumonia" (H. Weber).
Thus it is, that inflammatory affections of
the respiratory organs are more frequently a
cause of death in mountain districts than in
low lying ones. As has been noted under
the effects of altitude, the intense cold of the
Alpine winter does not seem to be an all-

important factor in the cure of the disease. The chief benefits from it being its power of causing (*a*) greater dryness of the atmosphere, and (*b*) greater purity of the air. The ground being covered continuously with snow, prevents all emanations from it, as well as the raising of dust; and the low temperature also diminishes the power of low organisms to grow and multiply. But to many constitutions it brings attendant evils, by depressing the vital functions of the weakly and by increasing the liability to inflammatory affections, thus neutralising much of the good such persons might otherwise have obtained through the other favourable agencies. Through what Dr. Denison has named the "diathermancy" of the air, the sun temperature in Alpine regions and on high elevations generally speaking, is relatively very high to the shade temperature, and absolutely so to that of places at a lower elevation. For Dr. Denison found by the researches he made in Colorado, that the sun's rays are transmitted with an increased facility through the rarified air of high altitudes, which causes an increased differ-

ence between the sun and shade temperature of 1° F. for every 235 feet in altitude.
But Volland has shown by comparison of
the results obtained at Davos and at
Strassburg, that it is only in winter that
there is this excess of sun temperature in
favour of the Alpine regions; for in summer
he found that it was greater at Strassburg
than at Davos.

(4). *Great purity of the air and its aseptic
condition* —For any place or climate to prove
efficacious in the treatment of phthisis,
purity of atmosphere, both from organic
and inorganic material, is essential. One
has only to look at the disastrous effects on
the lungs caused by certain trades and em-
ployments, to have ample proof of the
injurious and irritating action of dust on
the delicate air-passages ; thus there is coal-
miners' phthisis entirely brought on by the
constant inhalation of coal dust. Masons,
knife-grinders and others suffer in the same
way.

Now, great purity of the atmosphere is a
prominent character of both mountain and
sea air. In mountain districts this feature

is more marked during the winter than
during the summer season, for then not
only is there the same rarefaction of the air
allowing the particles of dust to be more
quickly precipitated from it, but the intense
cold—as has been mentioned above—diminishes the developing power of low organisms, and through its keeping the ground
continuously covered with snow, all noxious
emanations as well as all dust are prevented.

(5). *A rocky and dry subsoil.*—The Alpine regions are characterised generally
by a rocky subsoil, and provided that the
health resort is not situated on the peaty
and often boggy land at the bottom of
a valley too near the lakes or rivers, but
on a slope or slight elevation above the
base of the valley, as at Davos, St. Moritz
or Pontresina, the subsoil is, as a rule, remarkably dry. That this is a really important point in the treatment of phthisis,
has been proved by the fact that a damp
ill-drained subsoil has really a close connection with the development of phthisis,
not only in isolated instances, but in the
case of whole communities and districts.

Thus, as Dr. Buchanan has shown, the prevalence of phthisis has greatly diminished in Salisbury and other places since the improved system of drainage has been instituted.

(6). *A scanty and sparse population.*— That the overcrowding of dwellings and the aggregation of large masses of population are a fruitful source of consumption, is now well recognised; and the existence of only a scanty population is almost universally a characteristic of those districts which have an entire or comparative immunity from phthisis. In every country the mortality from phthisis in the country districts is smaller than in the towns, and it progressively increases in direct proportion to the density of the population. Also this is typically seen in the comparative rarity of the disease in mountainous districts, which are never thickly populated; as well as on the Tartar Steppes, and on the plains and deserts of Arabia and North Africa, inhabited only by Arabs and other nomadic tribes. Other factors, of course, such as occupation, altitude, a dry climate, and so

forth, also come into play in all these instances.

Having examined the characteristics of
the Alpine climate and their most apparent and important actions on the human
economy, let us now consider the indications and contra-indications for sending
patients to Davos and to other Alpine
resorts.   Though these have often been
discussed, yet considering the misappre-
hensions still existing on some of these
points and the manifestly inappropriate
cases sent there year after year, it may not
be amiss to restate them afresh.

Cases should be chosen with great care,
and invalids should not be indiscriminately
sent off to this climate without a clear and
definite examination of the patient's *constitutional* condition; for even after elimin-
ating many cases which are manifestly
inappropriate, there are many who are sent
there every year who should presumably do
well, and who yet derive harm instead of
good by a residence there.

The *general* constitutional indications for
sending patients to an Alpine winter,

are :—(*a*) that they must have good circulation ; (*b*) that they are able to bear
cold well ; (*c*) that they have a good general
physique ; (*d*) that they are comparatively
young ; persons under forty or so generally
doing very much better than those more
advanced in life. Children are an exception, however, for it is generally recognised
that sea air suits them better than keen
mountain air.

The opposite conditions to the above, as
well as other specific diseases or tendencies,
generally contra-indicate a residence in an
Alpine climate. Thus, it should be avoided
(1) by those who have weak circulations,
whether due to actual heart disease or not ;
(2) by those who suffer from or feel the cold
at home; (3) by those who are getting on in
life, and generally speaking by the weak
and infirm; (4) by those who have a liability
to inflammatory diseases ; (5) by those with
kidney disease ; or (6) by those with a tendency to brain affections such as epilepsy or
apoplexy.

Cases of catarrhal phthisis frequently do
better in a warmer climate. There seems a

tendency in the Alpine winter to induce albuminuria, and I have heard of several cases where profuse and persistent albuminuria has ensued on a residence at Davos. If this observation is borne out in any considerable proportion of cases, it will prove a disadvantage to the Alpine treatment.

The *special* indications for sending patients to Davos are :—

1. A predisposition to phthisis.

2. Convalescence from acute and exhausting diseases. It is especially useful in expanding the lung after pleurisy, and in stretching and neutralising the effects of old adhesions.

3. Cases in the first and second stages of phthisis, "those who have single cavities or limited consolidations; genuine primary phthisis comes round best " (one is tempted to ask, where is this not the case ?) ; "but on the other hand, those far advanced, with much fever and double cavities, not unfrequently do well " (C. Allbutt).

It is therefore very difficult to decide against allowing a patient to try a residence there; the great criteria to my mind being

the power of the circulation, and the liability
to intercurrent attacks of pleurisy or bronchitis. A poor circulation, with or without any
organic disease of the heart, being entirely
inimical to a residence in Alpine climates.
Dr. Burney Yeo, in his excellent work on
"Climate and Health Resorts," goes to the
root of the question when he says, "regard
must be had rather to the constitution and
temperament of the individual than to the
mere amount of local disease." It is most
painful to see some of the patients sent
there only to be literally killed. I know of
two cases sent by a London consultant in
one week, who both died from heart failure
within a few days of their arrival. One of
these, an elderly gentleman, remained in a
constant state of severe dyspnœa from the
time of his arrival until his death, which occurred within a few days; he never recovered from his rapid ascent, for he went
straight from London to Davos without a
break, and in the shortest possible time.
Now, surely, the condition of his heart as
well as of his lungs should have been examined and taken into consideration; for

if he had been sent to the Riviera or
Madeira, he would in all probability have
done well. If there had been any doubt
after carefully considering his case, and
yet on the whole the Alpine climate
seemed advisable, he should at all events
have been cautioned of the danger of
making a too rapid ascent.

4. General weakness and debility, or to
again quote Dr. Clifford Allbutt, " These
regions offer great curative advantages to
many others besides phthisical cases; pallid,
ill-nourished young men and women, and
older men and women overworked and worn
by care, cases of indefinite debility and
many others needing a stimulant to nutrition and change of scene and thought, and
to these many places are available ; but not
so to the phthisical, to them Davos has undoubtedly the advantage."

It is no great argument in favour of
Davos to say that a larger proportion of
cases sent there get cured than elsewhere ;
for it *ought* to have the best results and the
greatest percentage of cures from the very
class of patients sent ; in fact it would be

very bad if it were not so. It has a very unfair advantage, in this respect, over other warmer and less trying localities ; for, apart from the *stage* of the disease, which may be stated in statistics, it admittedly gets all the strongest cases—those with the best circulation, the best physique, the best digestion, and other favourable factors, all of which are conducive to recovery.

In the Alpine winter cure of phthisis there certainly seems a good deal of the "kill or cure" system. Not unfrequently sad, sudden and unexpected deaths occur in persons who would have in all probability continued to live for some years in a less trying climate ; while, on the other hand, real cures may sometimes be effected there, instead of the mere palliation, which might have been the effect in a less stimulating and invigorating climate.

This question, therefore, often presents itself:—Is it justifiable to run some risk with the hope of obtaining an absolute cure, just as it is right to urge a serious surgical operation in which there must necessarily be some risk incurred, but where there is

reasonable ground to hope for an ultimate
cure ? The answer seems to be that such
risk as does undoubtedly exist in some cases
may be ignored, if only the patients are not
urged to remain, but are ordered to descend
at once to a warmer climate if it does not
manifestly suit them. In this respect the
Maloja has a great advantage over Davos,
for the descent to the Italian lakes may be
made from the former at once, without the
difficulty and danger of a long coach or
sledge drive over some pass, as from the
latter.

The importance of constant medical
supervision in phthisis, at all events in its
more active stages, is, as a rule, scarcely
sufficiently recognised; but it is so at Davos,
to which fact I think some of the credit of
the place is due. As a certain fee is charged
for the season to those patients who put
themselves under the care of a local physician, all scruples of the medical man in
constantly looking in upon his patients,
whether sent for or not, to see if they are
doing well, are avoided ; and, not only so,
but the patient himself does not then feel

that the doctor is paying him what he often imagines to be unnecessary visits.

The plan in the Riviera is very different ; and it would be well if the physicians there, and in other similar resorts, would adopt the above plan as a working rule, though of course exceptional payment should be made in cases requiring an exceptional amount of care and treatment. As it is now, a napoleon is charged for a visit, and the invalid who has probably already been put to much expense and inconvenience in his business matters and so forth, endeavours to do as long as possible without calling in a doctor. Thus a slight relapse or catarrh is allowed to work mischief, and gain an firmer hold on the patient before the doctor is summoned. When one hears tales of the physicians charging a napoleon or a guinea for a casual word in the street, or on passing on the stairs of an hotel (this is a true fact, not a mere hearsay) a mere "how are you to day?" it is not to be wondered at, that patients who have to pay any attention at all to their expenses, and they are the vast majority, feel shy of call-

ing in the doctor till they are absolutely
obliged to do so.

The question whether a patient should
return home to England from Davos during
the summer is often discussed ; and it seems
a harder question to answer in reference to
Davos than to many other resorts. I have
known cases of phthisis which have improved rapidly, perhaps a stone weight
being gained, after returning to a comfortable English home from a sea voyage, or
after a winter spent in some much vaunted
foreign resort, where good and appropriate
food was not attainable, and the cooking
repulsive to an English palate. On the
other hand, one only too frequently hears of
the harm done to many patients by returning to our fickle English summer. Amongst
the physicians at Davos the rule apparently
is, that if the patient is doing really well
and improving nicely, he should not return
to England during the summer to run the
risk of losing the start he has obtained ; but
that if he has not improved, or is depressed
and despondent, it is best to let him have
the change home ; while at the same time

he should be urged not to relax the hygienic
discipline he has been kept under during the
winter.

It seems to me, however, that the decision
should always greatly depend, firstly, on a
patient's home surroundings—for instance
whether he lives in the town or country, in
a dry and healthy, or in a damp and unhealthy district; and, secondly, on the patient's own character and habits, *i.e.*, whether
he will probably be careful and continue the
daily strict routine impressed upon him by
his physicians, or whether he will enter into
doubtful amusements and over-exertion;
whether he can refrain from going to
picnics, and so forth, where he must incur
the risk of getting wet through in our
variable climate.

As to the questions, when should patients
take up their quarters in the Alps for
the winter, and whether they should
leave during the snow melting period in
the spring, there is some difference of
opinion. Nominally, the winter season
begins on the 1st of October and lasts till
the end of March, and patients are often

urged to commence their residence there not later than the first week in October, in order that they may become acclimatised before the winter cold sets in. However, many do not arrive till much later, not in-deed till the end of November, or even far into December; and this will probably be more frequently the case when the railway is open, as it will obviate the dangers of being snowed up on the way from Coire or Ragatz to Davos. By going up so late in the season their length of residence in the rarefied air of the Alps is of course short-ened, and too brief a period is left to confer much benefit in a disease such as phthisis, which requires so much time and patience for its amelioration. But I did not hear of any bad effects wrought on those who arrive so late in the season, while they escape a great deal of exceedingly bad weather during the on-coming of the winter, and before the real "snowing in" takes place. It is admitted also by the physicians that the chief bene-fit is obtained, and most cures effected, during the three months of January, Febru-ary and March. There seems, therefore, no reason why patients should not be sent up late in the season, if it is thought advisable on other grounds.

The fine and settled winter weather usually breaks up towards the end of March, when a large proportion of the invalids take their departure. Till the last few years this course has been recommended by the medical men there, but now their opinion is altering in this respect, and many patients remain during the melting time of the snow and the unsettled spring months without any detriment. One reason for this change of opinion seems to be the great difficulty of finding a really satisfactory place, and one which is sufficiently accessible, for patients to go to during this, the most trying time of the whole year. The Italian lakes, Montreux, Les Avants, Meran in the Austrian Tyrol, and other places, are recommended. As for myself, I tried Meran and found it most decidedly *wanting*. The winds were cold and strong, the dust simply awful, so that occasionally one could not see the houses on the opposite side of the road, and the whole landscape was blotted out with dense clouds of it. On one occasion this lasted for two or three consecutive days! However good, therefore, Meran may be as a winter resort, it is not a satisfactory place in spring, on account of the cold north winds which sweep down the valleys of the Adige and Passer, raising such clouds of dust, and which often bring snow low down on the mountains. Montreux and Les Avants, being so near such a large body of water as the Lake of Geneva, are considered rather too damp for those who have been accustomed to such a dry air as that of Davos. Invalids also frequently descend to Thusis and Ragatz, and stay there while the snow is melting on higher levels, or till they can return to England; these places are, however, undoubtedly unsatisfactory, as indeed is almost every locality in Central Europe during spring time, the most trying, windy, and unsettled time of the whole year.

Consequent on the recognised fact that elderly people do not do well at Davos, the majority of visitors and invalids are young persons, and therefore there is more gaiety, dancing, etc., in the hotels, and more active pursuits such as skating and tobogganning out of doors than in most health resorts, and the delicate are often induced prematurely to join in these hard exercises to their lasting harm. There can be no doubt that too great exertion is as harmful for the phthisical, on the one hand, as the falling into invalid habits is on the other.

The exertion, for instance, of dragging a toboggan up a long incline is very great, and while this ascent is very heating, the rushing down at the rate of half a mile a minute through the keen air is most chilling; so that though it may be an excellent exercise for the strong, it should not be indulged in by the phthisical without the precise sanction of his doctor. Very much the same may be said of the " dances," which are so much the fashion, except that they have the additional evils of being carried on in the close and necessarily vitiated air of the hotel rooms, and that the participators in them dress in much lighter clothing than they have been wearing during the day; then after becoming heated with the exercise in a room at a temperature of between 70° and 80° F., they go out in the night air at a temperature of zero.

It is impossible to keep some ladies away from this amusement, for if there is a dance taking place in any of the hotels, they will dance all the evening in spite of the doctor's strictest orders to the contrary and suffer for days after in consequence.

Some minor complaints have to be faced at Davos; while certain of these, such as chilblains and frost cracks (though it is sometimes denied that these are frequent, yet some persons who are not troubled with them during an English winter suffer from them there), are only disagreeable, there are other minor ailments which do retard the progress of some patients. Bad sore and ulcerated throats are far from being uncommon, an indication against sending patients there who are subject to inflammatory conditions of the throat.

Again, neuralgia and bilious attacks are very prevalent, and though perhaps not serious in themselves, are very disagreeable, and often retard the patient's progress.

English doctors, and English people generally, will understand what is meant by "bilious attacks," though many German physicians deny that there is such a complaint, and declare that Germans know no such ailment, and that if English people have a pain anywhere they put it down to "biliousness."

The choice of a room is most important, more so perhaps than in any other class of health resorts. It should always be firstly, a south room, and secondly, as large and airy as possible, with two windows if possible, as by these means ventilation can be so much more efficiently carried out without causing injurious draughts. Nowhere is good ventilation without draught more difficult; nor is there any place where it is more necessary, for the air in the rooms seems so quickly exhausted, and, to use an expressive term, they very rapidly become "stuffy."

It only remains now for me to say a few

words on the other popular neighbouring
Alpine winter resorts, viz., St. Moritz,
Wiesen, and the Maloja.

St. Moritz, as I have before incidentally
mentioned, is relatively much more exposed
than Davos, and is also nearly 1000 feet
higher, so that it is still keener than Davos.

Absurd as it may appear, I have heard
persons coming from St. Moritz complain
that Davos, with perhaps 20° F. of frost,
was *relaxing*, and that, therefore, they could
not do so much there as at St. Moritz!
Is not this a lesson to those at Davos not
to talk of the Riviera in the disparaging
way they do, on account of what they allege
to be its relaxing and debilitating influence?
St. Moritz from its greater altitude, its
greater degree of cold, and from its more
exposed condition is, therefore, still further
confined to the more robust and stronger
class of patients. The Maloja hotel affords
some advantages to the invalid (as has been
stated in Chapter I.) in the way of good
ventilation, the variety and fineness of its
reception rooms, the spaciousness of its
corridors, and the ease with which the

H

descent into Italy can be affected, but it has two disadvantages :—first, the windiness, and secondly, the lowness of its position, it being placed only a very few feet above the level of the lake, between which and the hotel is some marshy ground, though this is not so important during the winter as during the summer months.

Wiesen, situated in a valley eleven or twelve miles below Davos, and 350 feet lower, can never become a popular or large resort on account of its more confined space ; but it just affords that slightly greater degree of warmth and shelter which the more delicate patients may require, it being about as much more protected than Davos, as St. Moritz is more exposed.

FUNCHAL.—MADEIRA.

CHAPTER IV.

MADEIRA.

IT is scarcely surprising that Madeira has
been more or less neglected of late years
as a health resort for invalids, since the
very antithesis of the climatic treatment
obtained there, viz., that of sending patients
to the rigors of an Alpine winter, has become so popular, and of such proved efficacy in very many cases where phthisis
occurs in those with a good circulation and
strong physique.

It seems, however, to be felt, though perhaps yet scarcely acknowledged, that this
remarkable swing of the pendulum in the
medical treatment of phthisis has gone too
far; else why this rush to the Canary
Islands, why this anxiety to try their climate in such cases—a climate so very
similar to that of Madeira, and yet so very
dissimilar to that of Davos?

H 2

Madeira was at one time most popular as a health resort, but it has lately gone very much out of favour with the profession. The sending of a selected number of cases from the Brompton Consumption Hospital to pass a winter there, who unfortunately did not on the whole do well, seems to have helped to give the island its " coup de grace " for such invalids. This occurred some twenty years ago or more, just before the attention of English physicians was being drawn to the wonderful results said to be obtained by sending such cases to spend a winter at a high altitude, amongst the the snows of the Swiss Alps. Madeira, therefore, went more and more out of fashion as the Alpine treatment of phthisis came into fashion ; and by this great oscillation of medical opinion, cases for which the climate is eminently suited, have been sent to languish in the great cold of an Alpine winter.

At the present day but little seems known of the climate of Madeira amongst the medical profession at large. When a London specialist on this subject describes

the climate to be like the atmosphere of
the "hot and well-steamed room of a patient suffering from bronchitis," one can
see how little its real climate is known
and appreciated. That may be a very
good theoretical description of the climate,
but it certainly is not a correct one. Such
days as are here portrayed do occasionally
occur, and then the weather is very enervating; just as when the Föehn occurs in
Alpine districts, or when the so-called
Sirocco of Italy and the Mediterranean
blows, the visitors and inhabitants alike of
these districts feel enervated and depressed.
But to describe these conditions as the
normal state of the climate would be unfair
and misleading.

Again, Dr. More Madden, writing on the
climate of Madeira, says:—"The extreme
humidity of this climate is shown . . . . .
by the exuberant tropical vegetation which
attracts the admiration of every visitor to
this island, and which, as rain only falls in
small quantities and at very long intervals,
must be maintained by the excessive
humidity of the atmosphere."

This argument from the richness of the vegetation of Madeira is constantly used as a proof of the excessive humidity of the climate ; but, as a fact, no such conclusion necessarily follows, since in the first place, the richness of the vegetation is exaggerated, and in the second place, what there is can be accounted for without assuming that there is an excessive degree of humidity. The amount of rainfall during the winter months (October to March, 25 inches) is amply sufficient to keep vegetation green and flourishing in the moderate temperature which prevails during these months, namely, 63° F. ; while irrigation is constantly employed for growing crops during the rest of the year. Semi-tropical plants doubtless grow with luxuriance in the gardens of the numerous villas which surround Funchal, because they are incessantly cared for.

During the Madeira summer the growth of all plants that are not of a shrubby or arboreal nature, and therefore of a deeply rooting character, is almost entirely at a standstill for lack of moisture ; herbage is entirely burnt up, while ordinary garden

plants cannot exist without continual sup-
plies of water. These remarks of course
refer only to the lower parts of the island
which is the resort of invalids. On the
higher lands there is a much greater degree
of dampness, and mists are frequent from
the condensation of the moisture in the
atmosphere caused by the cooling effect of
the higher mountains upon the air.

The four and a half days at sea neces-
sitated in getting to this favoured and
delightful island will always be a stum-
bling block in the way of many an intending
visitor, more especially if he happens to be
an invalid ; and many would choose a less
suitable climate and all the fatigues of a
long railway journey rather than brave
those few days at sea, notwithstanding the
splendid vessels of the Castle and Union
Lines of Steam Ships in which they may
take their passage, and in which they will
find every comfort and convenience as far
as that is possible at sea.

What will be considered additional drawbacks by some, are :—that the language
spoken is Portuguese, a language known

by comparatively few people; that the
duties at the Custom House are very high;
and that there is only a weekly post with
England.   One, however, quickly gets used
to all these; the discomforts of the sea are
soon forgotten in the delicious sunshine and
balmy air; most necessities are cheap, and
after once landing, the Custom House acts
no longer as a nightmare, except to those
about to set up house-keeping on their own
account, and who are desirous of importing
articles of furniture; and mail day soon
seems to come round so quickly that it is
quite an effort to get one's letters off in
time, and one begins to wonder how people
manage when they have two or three mails
in and out *per diem.*

Madeira, as far as the invalid is concerned,
practically means its capital, Funchal, with
its suburbs stretching along the shores of
the lovely bay, and up the slopes of the
amphitheatre of mountains, which encircle
the valley in which the town lies.

As Funchal, with the bay on the shores of
which it is situated, faces nearly due South,
it obtains all the sunshine and warmth

possible during the winter months, and is
well protected from the cool Northerly
winds by the high and imposing range of
mountains which rise behind the valley to
a height of 4,000 feet, clothed nearly to their
summits with verdure. They are cultivated
on the lower levels with vineyards and with
the sugar cane, and then with patches of
various kinds of grain to a height of 2,000
feet, after which, instead of cultivated land,
there are plantations of pine and chestnut.
To the East, the bay is bounded by the cliffs
of Cape Garajao or Brazen Head, and to the
West, by the Ponta da Cruz, a few miles
beyond which tower the noble cliffs of Cape
Girâo, nearly 2,000 feet in height.

The landing from the steamers in small
boats is a disagreeable process, especially
in rough weather, as there is not only a
good way to row to and from the steamers,
but the boat is beached on the sloping
shore, and is then dragged up by oxen.
One may be a little splashed in the process,
but it is quickly and skilfully done, and little
harm is experienced even by an invalid.

In really rough weather the landing is

effected at the Pontinha, which now affords
a very sheltered place for disembarkation
since the new breakwater connecting the
Pontinha with the Loo rock has been built.
Though the streets are kept fairly clean and
are said to be vastly improved from what
they used to be, still they are narrow and
confined, and afford by no means desirable
promenades for invalids. They are well
drained by covered sewers, but unfortunately
this does not obviate the existence of many
a foul odour. They are, however, no worse
and very much better, in many cases, in this
respect than many continental towns. The
new Gardens and Constitution Square are
nice open spaces, easily accessible from the
hotels situated in the town ; and where the
band plays twice a week.

The water supply, though efficient in
quantity, must be declared, as far as drinking purposes are concerned, with the exception of one spring, decidedly defective in
quality. The best water, and the only supply which is really fit for drinking purposes,
is that obtained at the fountain close by the
Governor's Palace, and nearly all the English

and other foreign residents send there for
their drinking water. When the carriers
have to bring this water a long distance they
are not always to be trusted, and have been
known to get the water from inferior springs
on the way. This may be one way in which
typhoid fever, which is too common in
Funchal, is spread. Those, therefore, who
take villas for the season should be very careful as to whom they employ for this purpose,
and they should, moreover, for safety, boil all
their drinking water. If, after boiling, it is
passed through a carbon filter it loses its flat
and insipid taste. From the very position of
the spring, which is thus so much relied on,
and even though the water from it seems
really good, yet it must run a great chance
of pollution, as it has to traverse subter-
raneously the whole length of the town.

The roads and streets are paved with
rounded pebbles from the beach, which are
often known by the elegant term of " petrified
kidneys," and are generally much disliked
by pedestrians, especially by those given
to wearing very thin boots. There are
very few level pieces of road to be met with

around Funchal, in fact the new road to
Camara de Lobos is the only flat road there
is. This is a great drawback, for the invalid
especially, as the roads are all too rough
and too steep for any wheeled vehicles to be
used at all. Their place is, however, taken
by two very convenient but very slow
methods of conveyance, namely the hammock and the bullock carro or car. The
former is slung to a long pole which is
carried on the shoulders of two men, and is
a very easy and comfortable means of conveyance, tending perhaps to encourage too
much the lazy proclivities of the healthy,
but invaluable for the invalid who can thus
always obtain fresh air and passive exercise
without fatigue or over-exertion. It is
simply marvellous the distance and length
of time the bearers can continue to carry a
person in a hammock without having to
rest; and though they evidently find it very
trying for their "wind" up the steeper in-
clines, yet they deem it quite *infra dig.* to
rest, and appear quite offended at such a
proposal.

The bullock carro is drawn by a pair of

oxen and is capable of seating four persons;
though there are some smaller and lighter
ones for only two persons, which are generally used for the longer excursions out of
the town. They run like a sleigh instead of
on wheels, and though rather slow are safe
and comfortable, and run smoothly.

Riding horses are easily obtained, but all
the roads except the one above mentioned
(the new road—which is the favourite riding
road), being paved and mostly very steep,
the riding is decidedly trying for many invalids. Riding, indeed, in Madeira, is only
undertaken as a means to an end, *i.e.*, that
of getting about. It is not a pleasurable
exercise as in most countries; for one can
never go out of a walk, or amble, and even that
is jerking and disagreeable from the steep
paved roads, and the way the horses have
to be shod in consequence, to prevent them
from slipping—somewhat similarly to the
way horses are "roughed" in England in
frosty weather. Walking, too, for the same
reasons, and on account of the great heat
of the sun, and the narrow roads shut in
on either side by high stone walls, is unin-

teresting and tiring in the extreme. So
much the greater, therefore, is the importance of the position of his hotel to the invalid. The importance of this is scarcely
realised at home, nor perhaps by the casual
and healthy visitor, especially if he has been
accustomed to a town life ; but it is of primary importance to the invalid, when he
has to be imprisoned there for six or seven
months, and is forbidden to take long excursions, or is unable to do so from physical
weakness. A nice piece of garden, a level
shady road, or a prettily laid out public
park or garden near, and even a pretty and
interesting view from his rooms, or from
the verandah of the hotel then become
assessed at their true value.

This leads one to speak of the accommodation that Funchal provides for its visitors.
There are numerous villas or Quintas (pronounced Kinta) available for families, which
are let furnished by the season at reasonable prices, in good positions, and at various
elevations, which are a great convenience
for large parties. Plate and linen, however,
are not supplied, and these have to be

brought out by those who are intending to
take a house. But the majority of visitors
do not wish to go to the expense of a private villa, or to have the worry of foreign
servants, and all the other troubles setting
up housekeeping in a strange country in-
volves. To them, therefore, the hotel, its
position, its surroundings, and its management, are of primary importance; for on
these will greatly depend not only the comfort of, but also much of the benefit obtainable by, the invalid. Inferior food and bad
cooking often mean failure of appetite and
lack of due nourishment; while a bad position often means loss of exercise, a defi-
ciency of fresh air, a lack of interest, and
often, therefore, lowness of spirits and home
sickness.

Funchal has suffered in the past (just as
the Canary Islands are doing now) from the
position of the hotels; for I feel convinced
if they had been more judiciously placed in
the fresher and more airy outskirts of the
town, instead of in its narrow and hot
streets, so many complaints of the climate
being enervating, oppressive and relaxing,

would never have been heard. Without
entering into the merits of the several
hotels, I may say that all the proprietors
lay themselves out in a most unusual way
to meet the wants and requirements of invalids. Indeed, it is very rare to find in
any of the hotels of the many health resorts
of the Continent (and I speak from experience) such consideration and attention paid
to the invalid as is done here. The Santa
Clara is the largest and best known of the
hotels, and being in the town it is more central, but its situation is not so good for
those who come for health as either of
Cardwell's hotels, both of which are excellent in every way ; or Jones', which is also
in a good, open, and airy situation, with a
large garden.

All the food supplied is generally very
good, whether fish, flesh, or fowl. Fish is
plentiful and fresh, and rarely unobtainable,
but most kinds are rather tasteless in comparison with the fish of our cooler and shal-
lower seas. Both cows' and goats' milk are
obtainable in any quantities, the latter being
particularly nice and quite free from the

strong and disagreeable "goaty" flavour so generally associated with that animal's milk. The goats are milked at the door, so that it can be had two or three times a day quite fresh and warm. If taken this way it is certainly lighter and more easily digested. Fresh vegetables are always plentiful, and can be obtained all the year round, and resort has not to be made to tinned vegetables so often used on the continent. Fruit is always obtainable, and exists in wonderful variety. Bananas are always in season; strawberries are procurable from February far on into the summer; then oranges, loquats, figs, mulberries, the edible fruit of the Passion flower, grapes, pears, apples, plums, prickly pears (Opuntia tuna), guavas, avocado or alligator pears (Persea gratissima), mangoes, custard apples (Annona reticulata), pomegranates, and the Cape gooseberry, all come in their season. Amongst the other advantages of Funchal, are the splendid English library and reading-rooms. I know of no foreign resort which has their equal, and they are a great resource and rendezvous for visitors.

Mosquitoes are said to be entirely absent,

I

but this certainly is not the case. They are, however, not so numerous, and are never a pest, as in the Riviera or in Las Palmas.

The climate of Madeira has been a great deal discussed in past years, and much variety of opinion has been expressed upon it, one calling it enervating and depressing, and "like the steamy air of a patient's room who is suffering from bronchitis;" while another authority speaks of it as " La première résidence hivernale du monde;" and the late Sir James Clark speaks of it in much the same terms. There is much variety, too, in the results obtained by observers, which is due (1) to the variety of instruments used; (2) to the district, and altitude of that district, in which the observations have been taken; (3) to the number of seasons which the record covers—an abnormally hot or cold, an unusually dry or wet season, influencing the mean of three or four years' observations very materially; but (4) and chiefly, the variations are caused by the *position* of the instruments. For instance, there is a considerable difference between the readings of a thermometer placed in a shady verandah looking North, or on a cool North wall, to one placed in a Stevenson's screen with the full blaze of a hot sun upon it, as is the regulation of the Royal Meteorological Society of England; while the former seems generally accepted as the best position for amateur observers who do not care to be encumbered with a large screen on their travels. Now, as the difference between the maximum readings in these different situations may be several degrees, while the minimum will vary but little, it accounts to some extent for the exaggerated idea which obtains as to the great equability of the temperature as regards the daily range, which H. Weber gives as only from 7° to 9° F.; Heineker and Renton, for six years' observations, give it as varying from 10° to 11° F.; while I make it for the seasons of 1888 and 1889, nearer 12° F. Thus, with Casella's instruments, Kew certificated, and placed in a regulation Stevenson's screen, the average minimum for March 1889 was 54° F., and the mean maximum 66·7° F., giving a mean daily range for the month of 12·7° F. Again,

the average minimum for April, 1889, was
54·5° F., and that of the maximum 67·3° F.,
or a difference of 12·8° F.

For the last twenty-three years the reports taken at the Official Meteorological
Office in Funchal are available, and the
following particulars, as published by Mr.
Yate Johnson in his handbook for Madeira,
are taken from that source as being more
uniform, and covering a longer period than
the results obtained by other private observers. The mean daily range is there
given as 9·4° F. The mean annual temperature, according to the official returns
for the nineteen years, 1865 tò 1883, is
65.7° F.; but this is not of much value from
the medical point of view ; for a place with
a very hot summer and very cold winter,
i.e., a locality with great extremes of temperature, may give a mean annual temperature very similar to another with a cool
summer and warm winter temperature, and
yet the climates are really a great contrast.
Thus the mean annual temperature ot
Dublin, for instance, is 48·4° F. ; while
that of Odessa is 49·3° F.—within less than

a degree of difference ; and yet the mean winter temperature of Dublin is 41˙4° F., while that of the latter is 28˙2° F., or 13˙2° F. colder, and the summer is correspondingly hotter. When compared with the health resorts of the Riviera we find the mean annual temperature of Madeira only 4˙7° F. warmer than that of Mentone, which is 61° F. ; while the winter temperature is about 10° F. (10˙2°) warmer, and the summer temperature correspondingly cooler.

During the nineteen years from which these figures are taken, viz., 1865 to 1883, the highest temperature recorded was 90˙5° F. in July, 1882 (a temperature not unfrequently exceeded in England), and the lowest was 45 6° in March 1883, which is the lowest temperature ever recorded in Funchal. February is the coldest month, with a mean temperature of 60˙3° F., being ˙18° F. colder than January and March. These three months, therefore, have an almost identical mean temperature of about 60˙4° F. August and September are the warmest months, with the means of 72˙8° F. and 72˙3° F. respectively.

The mean temperatures for the four
seasons are as follows :—winter (December, January, February) 60·9° F. ; spring
(March, April, May) 62·6° F. ; summer
(June, July, August) 70·5° F. ; and autumn
(September, October, November) 68·9° F.
The most noticeable points about the climate as regards temperature, are :—(1)
the small mean difference between succes-
sive months, which is only about 2° F. ;
(2) the steadiness of the temperature from
day to day ; for instance, sometimes neither
the maximum nor the minimum will vary
more than a couple of degrees for a week
or more together ; (3) the small range of
temperature in the 24 hours, which may be
taken as about 10° F. to 11° F. ; though if a
Stevenson's screen is used as in England,
and as above explained, it is probably
greater, for I have frequently seen it amount
to 15° F., and but rarely to less than 10° F.

The fall of temperature at sunset is very
small but very regular. I have found from
numerous observations taken by a thermometer four feet from the ground, in the
open, and protected only from the sun's

declining rays, that the average fall from half an hour before sunset till sunset is 2° F., that from sunset to half an hour after it is 1·5° F., and that during the next half hour, from half an hour till an hour after sunset, the fall is only ·4° F. It will, therefore, be seen that the greatest fall is before sunset, and there is no sudden fall immediately afterwards, as in the Riviera.

The mean annual rainfall for these years is given as 26·02 inches, varying from 12·93 inches in 1868, to 49·14 inches in 1867. This mean total fall, however, is probably rather understated, and Dr. Grabham's estimate of 29 inches seems nearer the truth; for the rain gauge at the Meteorological Office is very badly placed. Not only is it put on the top of a building at least 40 feet from the ground, but it is also not sufficiently free from surrounding buildings, a turret rising high above it on one side at only a short distance from it. According to season the rain fell as follows :—winter, 11·31 inches; spring, 5·64 inches; summer, 1·24 inches; and autumn, 7·82 inches. The months of July and August are practi-

cally rainless, and not unfrequently no rain
falls in June and September.

The mean annual number of days on
which rain was registered was 78. Snow is
often seen on the mountains ; but it never,
or only very rarely, falls below a height of
2500 feet, at least to lie.

The relative humidity is generally considered to be about 72 per cent. The official records for the eleven years 1873 to
1883 (inclusive), taken at 9 a.m. and 3 p.m.,
give a mean of only 64·3 per cent.

Another record taken at the same hours
for the years 1865 to 1872, gives it as 69·1 per
cent. The two factors which influence the
humidity of the air most, are :—firstly, the
"Leste" which reduces it to an abnormally
small percentage, and secondly, on the
other hand, the occurrence of S.W. or
Westerly winds which cause almost complete saturation.

Clouds are a very prominent feature of
the climate, and an unclouded sky throughout the day is a rare occurrence, but the
nights are as a rule far more cloudless than
the days. It is stated that dew never falls

in Madeira, but this is certainly a mistake; I have often observed it, especially during the autumn months, after a clear night. The amount of cloud is large, half the sky being on an average constantly covered. But as the clouds are chiefly to the North, they do not intercept as much sunshine as might have been anticipated. They are of an irregular cumulus nature, or strato-cumulus, and sometimes what has been termed roll-cumulus, but rarely of the true trade-cumulus character. The diverging rays of the sun which stream down from behind clouds like a fan, and which often produce a beautiful effect, and about which there are many diverse legends in various parts of the world, are often observed shortly before sunset in Madeira. They are not very commonly seen in England, and when seen the sun is said to be " drawing water." In Ceylon, these are called " Buddha's rays," and in the Pacific Islands they are called the " Ropes of Maui," the latter being the great hero of the Pacific Islanders, who caught the sun and noosed him with his ropes!

Mists, except on the mountains, are very

uncommon, but occasionally one gets a sea
mist driving in with a warm westerly wind.
The sunsets are frequently very beautiful,
especially during the winter months when
the sun sets to seaward.

The barometrical pressure is remarkably
uniform, the mean pressure being as nearly
as possible 30 inches, but the diurnal oscilla-
tions are well marked. Mr. Yate Johnson
states that the maximum pressure during the
eight years 1865 to 1872 was 30·554 inches,
and the minimum 29·083 inches; the entire
range being therefore no more than 1·471
inches, so far as was revealed at the hours
of observation. The highest barometrical
reading I have observed during the year
1888-1889 is 30·45° F., and the lowest
29·54° F. (corrected to sea level), showing a
total range of only ·91 inch during the year.

Not only is the barometer remarkably
steady in the calm belt of Cancer in which
Madeira is situated (lat. 32° 43′), but its mean
height in these latitudes is higher than almost anywhere else, which is due to the
ncreased pressure caused by the meeting of
the polar and equatorial currents of air in

the upper regions of the atmosphere. The cool polar current then descends on the equatorial side of the calm belt to form the North-East trade winds, while the warm air which has risen in the tropics also gradually descends, and continues its course polarward in the form of the South-West winds or counter trades.

As I have just stated, Madeira is situated in the calm belt of Cancer, yet it obtains the benefit of the trade winds during the summer months, rendering the climate then a comparatively cool one, notwithstanding that the shores of the Island are washed by a branch of the Gulf Stream.

The North-East trade winds vary in the latitude at which they commence to blow at this season of the year, *i.e.*, with the position of the sun, commencing in a much higher latitude during the northern summer than during the winter; yet Madeira would scarcely get the true trade winds even during the summer months, if it were not for a special fact. This is that the North-East trade winds commence to blow from a much higher latitude on the Western margins of the Pacific and Atlantic Oceans, than in the more central and eastern portions. Thus, these winds commence to blow off the coast of Portugal in as high a latitude as 40° or 42° during the spring and summer months; and though this wind does not extend far out into the Atlantic, yet it embraces the Island of Madeira.

From these winds commencing off the coast of Portugal, they are known to sailors as the Portugese trade winds.

During the winter months the true trade winds commence south of Madeira, and though the North-East is still the prevailing wind there, it does not blow with the same regularity as in the spring and summer. It, however, brings the driest and finest weather to Funchal, as any excess of moisture it contains is condensed in its passage over the mountains, and reaches the south side of the Island as a comparatively dry and bracing air, without the trying direct effect of the trade winds, as is experienced for instance, in Las Palmas in Grand Canary.

The North and North-West winds are cool, and often blow up rain and snow on the mountains, and squally weather in the winter, but do not cause the great humidity of atmosphere which occurs with a Westerly wind. This is a warm wind, and does not blow for more than a few days together as a rule. Though it blows only on a small percentage of days, it seems to have given to Madeira a bad name in England ; for it is undoubtedly this wind which has given the island its character for being enervating and depressing. Yet the comparatively cool, bracing and dry (as it reaches Funchal) North-East wind largely preponderates.

Though this North-East wind is not by nature a dry one, yet after having risen over the high chain of mountains in the centre or the Island, where much of its moisture is condensed, it descends again into the valley of Funchal as a comparatively dry wind, with a relative humidity of only about 65 per cent.

There remains for me to mention the " Leste," which occasionally blows from the East or South-East. It is an extremely hot, dry and parching wind : thus differing very materially from what the Italians call a Sirocco, to which it has been likened ;

for that is a hot, damp and enervating wind, a great contrast to the "Leste" of Madeira. It far more resembles the Sirocco of Algeria or the Harmattan which blows over the Cape de Verde Islands carrying quantities of dust with it, to such an extent as to cause what is known as the red fogs of that district. This "Leste" arises on the heated deserts of Africa, where, as the air becomes heated and expanded, it rises in whirlwinds into the air, carrying with it quantities of sand and dust to be borne along by it hundreds of miles out to sea above the cooler North-East trade current. It then gradually descends far out in the Atlantic, and is experienced as a hot, dry and often boisterous wind in Madeira and the Canaries, and is often felt more severely on the higher mountains of the islands than in the districts near the sea. The highest temperatures recorded are registered during the continuance of this wind; but even a severe one will rarely raise the temperature over 90° F.; and it generally lasts only three days. It is only severe ones that are at all trying, and they rarely occur;

for being generally tempered by the cooler substrata of air they only cause a pleasant sensation of dry warmth. The discomfort of them has, I think, been greatly exaggerated; for though I have only been in Madeira between one and two years, I have experienced one of the worst that has occurred for several years; the temperature then reached about 92° F. for two days, and the minimum did not go below 71° F. The air instead of being exceptionally *free* from dust, as has been stated, is I believe loaded with impalpable, it may be, but veritable dust. Hence the lovely sunsets frequently experienced at these times,* as well as the remarkable haze which exists. A direct proof also of the presence of fine dust in the air is occasionally seen in the deposit of a thin layer of dust, not only on the

---

* These unusually brilliant sunsets have been ascribed to electrical phenomena, but from the researches entered into by the Royal Society and the Royal Meteorological Society as to the effects of the great Eruption of Krakatoa, it seems more probable that they are due to impalpable dust floating in the atmosphere.

island, but on the decks of ships far out
at sea.

It is a very curious fact that Professor
Ehrenberg, of Berlin, has found that this
" sea-dust," as it has been termed, collected
from ships in the Atlantic, from the Cape de
Verde Islands, and even from Malta, Sicily
and the mountains of the Tyrol, contained
infusoria and diatoms whose habitat is not
Africa but South America! Dr. Maury con-
siders this a direct proof " that there is a
perpetual upper current of air from South
America to North Africa."   Mr. Yate
Johnson states that he found six species
of diatoms in the dust which fell in Madeira
on one occasion, after a cessation of a Leste
or hot wind.   But he adds, that " all the
recognised specimens belong to species
which are found in every part of the world."

It is curious in the face of such facts as
these that Dr. Hermann Weber, in his
standard work on climate, should state :—
" Whilst it (the Leste) lasts, the air is remarkably *free* from dust, and contains a considerable amount of ozone."   Again, I have
found the direct contrary with regard to the

presence of ozone; for it is at these times almost entirely absent according to my observations. The sky is unusually free from clouds, and the air remarkably dry; not unfrequently the relative humidity falls to from 30 to 35 per cent., and Dr. Grabham mentions one occasion in which it was only 22 per cent.

Thunderstorms are very uncommon in comparison with England and the continent of Europe.

During the whole year from June 1st, 1888, to June 1st, 1889, there were only two thunderstorms; on one occasion there was distant thunder, and on another there was some sheet lightning without any thunder. When thunderstorms do occur, it is generally with a South-West or West wind, especially on the breaking up of the summer drought by the first rains of autumn.

Ozone I have found exists to a fairly large amount, on the average to nearly 3, on a scale of 0-10, but the quantity during the night is usually greater than during the day, in the proportion of 3·3 to 2·4.

Dr. Tucker Wise gives the average

amount for the Engadine as 7‧4 on a scale of
0 to 20.   The largest proportion by far exists
in the air during the humid westerly winds ;
less during the North-East winds ; while it
is almost entirely absent during a " Leste."

Though Madeira has been a well-known
and popular winter resort for the last fifty
years and more, yet, as I have intimated at
the beginning of this chapter, for the last
half of that period it has been declining in
fame as a resort for consumptives, unless
they are in an advanced stage of the disease ;
more especially has this been the case since
the heroic treatment of phthisis by the
Alpine winter cure came into fashion.
From being perhaps over-rated as a health
resort, it has become too much neglected
for certain cases of phthisis, which presumably should do well there, as well as for
other diseases, such as some forms of
bronchitis with irritable cough, or when
complicated with emphysema, which almost
invariably do well in this climate.

The character of the climate being essentially sedative, it is very suitable for cases of
laryngeal catarrh and chronic bronchial

catarrh, especially with a dry irritable mucous membrane. Cases of albuminuria and Bright's disease, where it is important to keep the skin active, and where chills and sudden checks to its action are injurious, do well, as these results are obtained to a remarkable degree by the equable climate. It is asserted, however, by some authorities that Bright's disease is peculiarly common amongst the natives.

As to the cases of phthisis in which the climate is likely to prove beneficial, those of an inflammatory nature with a tendency to bronchial or other intercurrent complications, except where there is a tendency to diarrhœa, are likely to do best; or those with poor circulations, who cannot stand a cold climate. Again, it is said to be wonderful how persons with advanced disease, but where it is not very active, are often able to lead a very comfortable, though of course quiet life in Madeira, whereas they could not exist at Davos, and scarcely so even in the Riviera. It is, however, doubtful how far it is right at any time to send advanced cases away from their

own people and their home surroundings.
This climate does not seem to be nearly as
effectual in checking cases of primary tubercular deposit, and in removing such consolidations, as the Alpine climate.

Pulmonary tubercular disease is comparatively seldom seen amongst the upper
classes of the Portuguese; but amongst the
poor in all districts it is not uncommon
(Grabham). There is a remarkable mildness in all inflammatory diseases; but diarrhœa is often severe amongst the natives,
and causes a great mortality amongst the
children of the poor. Visitors also often
suffer from it, especially if they are located
in the town itself; but it does not seem as
general or as severe as amongst the visitors
to the Canaries. It may be avoided or rendered only slight and tractable, if it is taken
in time, and if due precautions are taken till
the visitor is acclimatised, in avoiding too
much exposure to, and over-exertion in the
sun, in being careful and moderate in the
use of fruit, meat, and wine, and above all
in guarding against the opposite condition
during the voyage.

Typhoid fever is far from uncommon, but is not usually of a severe character, though occasionally it becomes virulent, both amongst the natives and visitors; and not unfrequently there are sad and unexpected deaths amongst the latter from it. But Funchal, unfortunately, is not singular amongst foreign, or indeed English, health resorts in these sad disasters, which are due either to bad drainage or to the contamination of the water supply, as I have before stated.

When typhoid occurs amongst the visitors in Funchal, it seems usually due to the very defective drainage of some of the villas, and every visitor who intends taking a Quinta for the winter, would be wise in obtaining some guarantee as to the condition of the drainage and water supply for flushing purposes, before making any agreement. If every one would take the trouble, in their own interest, thus to protect themselves, then pressure might be brought to bear upon the owners to put their houses in a sanitary condition. As it now is, even if one person, having made inquiries, refuses to take a certain house on account of its

insanitary condition, the next applicant is
probably led into taking it, perhaps with
disastrous results to his own family, and
therefore increasing the bad reputation of
the island in this respect.   Again, even
if the water used for drinking purposes is
supposed to be pure, it should for safety be
both boiled and filtered.

Funchal has, however, no mean advantages in other respects ; firstly, in the
good accommodation obtainable at moderate charges, whether in the hotels or in
private villas, and the much more kindly
attention received at the former by invalids, than in many places ostensibly known
as health resorts, which should certainly
be taken into consideration if patients
have to leave the comforts of their own
homes ; secondly, in the good food obtainable ; thirdly, in the entire absence of dust,
and the very slight amount of smoke (and
that chiefly wood smoke) ever present.
This absence of dust is due to the roads
all being paved, so that it is not formed
as on macadamised roads.   How different
from Egypt or the Riviera in winter, or the

Engadine in the summer! Lastly, in its southern aspect, whereby it obtains so large a proportion of sunshine, which enables the invalid to be out so much more in the fresh air than in resorts with a northern aspect, or at Davos, where the average sunshine is only 113 hours per month during the winter, and where the patient can rarely be out more than four hours a day.

Two or three weeks often pass in Madeira without a wet day during the winter; and it is most rare to have a day without at least some sunshine. In fact, during the six months from November to April, 1889, there were only nine days on which there was less than one hour of sunshine. Thus it is quite rare to experience a day when an ordinary invalid is not able to get out for at least some part of the day. Again, Funchal is far better protected from the cold North and North-East winds than Las Palmas or Orotava, which face East and North respectively, and where the winds in winter are often felt too trying for invalids to sit out in.

Winter in Madeira is truly avoided, not merely mitigated as in the Riviera; and the

cold North and North-East winds of continental Europe are warmed by passing
over a thousand miles of sea, itself warmed
by the great Gulf Stream.

From the researches of the " Challenger "
it was shown that the temperature of the
sea around Madeira is 72° F., which is
greatly above the mean temperature of the
atmosphere, and decidedly warmer than at
the Canary Islands, where it is only 69° F.,
though so much South of Madeira.

Till Madeira is reached, it is vain to look
for an immunity from those cold winds of
spring which are always so trying to the
invalid and to the weakly.

No doubt Madeira cannot show such
good statistics of recoveries from phthisis
as the Alpine resorts ; for admittedly all the
strongest cases, and those with every advantage in their favour, to say nothing of
the stage of the disease, are sent to Davos
and St. Moritz ; while Madeira is reserved
chiefly for those of weaker physical constitution, or for those who have some unfor-
tunate complication.   Is it fair to compare
the statistics of the two ?

The summer in Madeira is remarkably cool for its latitude, which is 32° 43', or much South of Tunis and Tripoli, and very much about the same latitude as Morocco or Alexandria. Yet it is rarely oppressive, and the thermometer does not often rise over 80°, even in the hottest month, except when a "Leste" is blowing, when the temperature may approach 90° for a day or two.

Many of the villas situated on the cliffs overlooking the sea on either side of the town are kept quite pleasantly cool throughout the summer by the fresh sea breezes, and thus even the heat of summer is not felt too trying, if it be thought advisable for the patient not to return to England. Unfortunately the higher stations in the island are mostly too damp, on account of their liability to be enshrouded in mists and clouds which so frequently gather on the mountains ; so that even the favourite and pretty district of Camacha, at a height of 2200 feet, does not altogether escape, even in summer. Much more is this the case, however, with the district around the Mount Church, which is nearly 2000 feet high, and where mists so constantly gather that the climate is quite unfitted for invalids. Neither Sanatorium again is of sufficient height in this latitude to give the benefit obtainable from the rarefied air of a true mountain climate; though after living in Funchal they are comparatively bracing.

The following table gives the rainfall, number of days on which rain fell, the number of days when there was less than one hour of sunshine, and the approximate number of hours of bright sunshine for the season of 1888-9. The season was an unusually dry and fine one, and though the sunshine given may be slightly above what a sun recorder would have registered, yet on subsequently comparing similar observations with the records of a Jordan's Sun Recorder, taken simultaneously, they seem fairly correct.

The natural tendency of such observations is to over-estimate the sunshine, but on clear days there is somewhat of an unavoidable discrepancy through the instrument not recording the first and last twenty minutes (or thereabouts) after the sun has risen, and before it sets respectively, though it is shining full upon the instrument. The automatic recorder has only been used for the following table since September 15th, 1889.

The rainfall for 1889, from January to November, was only 9·45 inches, or including December, 1888, to complete the year, it has been only 12·15 inches.

MONTH.	RAINFALL.	No. OF DAYS ON WHICH RAIN FELL	HOURS OF SUNSHINE.		NUMBER OF DAYS WITH LESS THAN 1 HOUR SUNSHINE.
1888.			Hrs.	Min.	
August . .	·00	0	*		*
September .	·725	6	*		*
October . .	3·035	12	171		3
November .	1·80	11	190	30	0
December .	2·70	13	194	30	0
1889.					
January . .	·64	10	185	30	2
February . .	1·59	8	166		3
March . . .	1·78	7	204		3
April . . .	·54	5	176		1
May . . .	1·35	8	133	45	2
June . . .	·48	3	*		*
July . . .	·05	1	*		*
August . .	·09	1	*		*
September .	1·36	5	117	35+	0
October . .	1·06	8	162		0
November .	·51	5	178	30	1

* Not recorded.

† Recorded by a Jordan's Sun Recorder from Sept. 15th only.

CHAPTER V.

A Winter in the Canary Islands.

These islands have been but little known to the English in the past, although only two hundred and fifty miles South of Madeira; but they have lately come very prominently into notice, partly through the opening up of improved communication with the islands, and partly through the writings of Mrs. Stone, who was the first English person to thoroughly explore and describe the islands, and to acquaint the public with the results of her travels there, in her excellent work on " Teneriffe and its six Satellites."

The medical profession, as well as the general public, have since shown a great deal of interest in the islands, and large numbers of people have visited them during the last three years. Many inquiries are also being made as to what prospect these islands have of affording a desirable winter resort for those who require a warmer and

VILLA ORATAVA AND PEAK OF TENERIFFE.

more equable climate than the Riviera, and
yet a drier one than that of Madeira.

There have already been several rather
acrimonious disputes in various periodicals
between the partisans of these Islands, and
those who consider themselves victimised in
being induced to pay the islands a visit,
through what they consider the too glowing
and too highly coloured descriptions of their
scenery and climate, which have so much
attracted public attention of late. Unfortunately instead of tending to settle the
matters in dispute, these discussions generally terminate in personalities, those writing
in favour of the islands being accused of
being interested in the various new hotels
springing up there, while those who see the
drawbacks connected with them, and which
undoubtedly exist, are at once judged to be
looking at everything with the jaundiced eye
of the chronic grumbler or dyspeptic!

Having spent seven months in the islands
as an invalid, my experiences may not be
devoid of interest to those who are inquiring
as to their suitability for invalids.

The island of Teneriffe may be most

quickly reached and with the greatest comfort by the fine ocean steamers of either Messrs. Shaw, Savill, and Co., or of the New Zealand Shipping Company, both of which sail monthly from London, and call at Plymouth, from which port they take only from four-and-a-half to five days. The intermediate steamers of the Castle Line of Packets to the Cape call at Grand Canary once a fortnight. The British and African and the African Companies' ships sail weekly from Liverpool, calling both at Teneriffe and at Grand Canary, and take about nine days on the voyage. These are smaller, slower and cheaper boats than the above mentioned, and vary much in their accommodation, some being clean and good, while others are dirty and uncomfortable. As they are the only lines of English steamers going to our possessions on the West Coast of Africa they are also apt to be overcrowded at certain times of the year. A weekly steamer service having lately been established between the islands to replace the old schooners, communication between the islands is now greatly facilitated.

The landing place and port of Las Palmas and for the Island of Grand Canary, generally, is at Puerto de Luz, some four miles from the town of Las Palmas itself, as a promontory, called the Isleta, forms a . more sheltered roadstead than the anchorage off Las Palmas. Even here the landing has to be effected in small boats, and is often made with difficulty on account of the heavy swell which generally prevails. The promontory is joined to the mainland by a narrow isthmus composed entirely of immense banks of sand. There is an excellent macadamised, but exceedingly bare, dusty and uninteresting road from Port de Luz to Las Palmas, and the supply of dust is always kept up most efficiently from the barren ground of the hills, and from the large banks of sand which line the road on either side!

The Canary Islands possess a great advantage over Madeira (and many other foreign resorts), in that they are all free ports, and one has not the aggravation of being charged by a set of voracious officials a heavy duty on the cost of all articles sent out from England.

I landed at Las Palmas with several other invalids about the middle of October, but we all found the heat still very oppressive, and we felt it would be better for invalids not to arrive in the islands before the beginning of November, unless they go to the high station of Laguna in Teneriffe, which has elevation of 2000 feet.

Las Palmas, the capital of Grand Canary, faces nearly due East, and is built on a flat strip of land at the base of some barren hills, and lies between them and the sea. It has a very Eastern appearance, as most of the houses are built in the Moorish style, with flat roofs and a central court or square called the " Patio," which is open to the sky and is often prettily planted with flowers and shrubs, and sometimes has a fountain playing in the centre.   The hotels at Las Palmas afford fairly good accommodation, though invalids have not hitherto been much considered, in fact have rather been thought " de trop."   There are two English hotels besides the Spanish Fonda, but the great complaint against them is that they are all essentially badly situated for invalids, being placed more or less in the streets of a particularly noisy, dirty and odorous town ; neither is it possible within an easy walk, to get out of these narrow streets for the fresh and pure air and the gentle exercise which is so essential to the phthisical. Certainly there are two Plazas in the city, in the principal of which, the Alameda, the band plays two or three times a week; but they are both far too small to afford any fresh air or sense of freedom from the surrounding streets. All invalids used, therefore, to drive almost daily to the fine sandy beach about a mile and a half off—a quite unattainable distance on foot for invalids in the hot sun experienced there—and spend the morning on the shore. Often, however, as there was no shelter of any kind to be obtained, the more susceptible of the invalids found the strong and cool North-East trade wind, which blows so persistently, too much for them, and they had to return to the close atmosphere of the town and hotel rooms. This sandy beach affords the best bathing place I

have seen in either of the islands or in
Madeira. The shore is shelving and the
water is beautifully clear, and never too
cold for those in health, though the swell is
sometimes too heavy for ladies to bathe
with safety. The temperature of the sea
is never below 64° F. The "Challenger"
reports give the temperature of the sea in
the Canary Archipelago as 69° F.

As there are no villas to be obtained,
as in Madeira or in the Riviera, every-
one is obliged to take up their quarters
in the town hotels. Until, therefore, there
is accommodation with good sanitary arrangements provided away from the streets
of the town, with gardens, sheltered bal-
conies and such like conveniences for the
delicate, so that they can obtain fresh air
without constantly inhaling the foul odours
of the streets of a drainless town, Las
Palmas does not seem to fulfil the element-
ary requirements of a health resort. Indeed,
from the amount of illness there during the
season 1887-1888 amongst the visitors, especially diarrhœa, typhoid and "bilious"
fevers, the first of which almost universally

attacks all new comers, whether healthy
or delicate, whether they are indiscreet in
their use of fruit or never touch it, it appears scarcely a satisfactory winter resort
for anyone; and many and great have been
the disappointments of those who have gone
with the expectation of spending a pleasant
winter, and of returning home in improved
health.

A large and fine hotel and sanatorium is
being built between the port and the town,
which is to be opened for the season
1889-90, and though its position is vastly
better than that of the other hotels, yet it is
too near the high road in front, and the
arid hills behind, and too exposed to the
prevailing winds. It is no doubt in a convenient and good position for business
people or for visitors in health, but before
Grand Canary can be looked upon as a
desirable health resort for invalids, a more
satisfactory spot than the windy, dusty and
populous town of Las Palmas, must be
discovered and opened up.

That the climate of Las Palmas is a
remarkably dry one there can be no doubt,

and this is more especially noticeable as it is an island and not a continental climate. During the six months from November 1888 to April 1889, only six inches of rain fell, and the relative humidity was only 65 per cent. This too is the rainy season of the year. The bright sunshine as registered by a Jordan's Sun Recorder for the same period, was as follows:—November 166 hours, December 129, January 137, February 167, March 193, April 140, or an average of five hours nine minutes per diem (Dr. J. Cleasby Taylor), against an average of only four hours seven minutes at Orotava, and six hours six minutes at Funchal (approximate). The above season was, however, an exceptionally fine and sunny one at the latter place.

The climate at Las Palmas may, therefore, be looked upon as a drier and more stimulating one than that of either Orotava or Funchal.

Leaving Grand Canary at the end of November, I spent the remainder of the winter in the Island of Teneriffe. The steamers take about six hours, or frequently a night, in going from Las Palmas to Santa Cruz, the chief town and port of Teneriffe, and the capital of the Archipelago. There are two fair hotels at Santa Cruz, but they labour under the same disadvantages as those of Las Palmas, and few persons stay there more than a day or two, as they hurry on to the more attractive places, Laguna and Orotava. I hear, however, an English boarding house, has been opened this season, a short distance away from the town. Though at present neglected, it seems probable that for the months of January, February and March, Santa Cruz, of all the places at present available for visitors, has the best climate in the islands; for as it has a southern aspect, the clouds which so constantly gather in these islands and form a perfectly thick, impenetrable canopy over the whole zenith, do not intercept so much of the sunshine as in those places, such as Orotava, which are situated on the North side. Again, it is more protected from the cool North-East winds to which the latter places are exposed, which are grateful enough later on in the

spring, but which are rather trying to many
invalids during the earlier months of the
year. No doubt, eventually, localities at
higher elevations, with a more bracing air
and yet above the " lie " of the clouds, will
be opened up. Villa Flor on the south side
of the island, at a height of 4500 feet, is said
to be such a locality ; but at present there
is no accommodation there whatever. The
clouds as a rule occupy an elevated band of
from 2500 feet to 3500 or 4000 feet, and one
may occasionally catch a pretty glimpse
through the heavy mass of clouds, of the
bright sunshine on the more elevated mountains, or on the peak itself. These clouds
come down so low occasionally as to make
living at the Villa Orotava very depressing.
From Santa Cruz to Orotava is a long six
or seven hours' drive, the road passing
through Laguna, above referred to, at a
height of nearly 2000 feet. The road com-
mences to rise almost immediately after
leaving Santa Cruz, ascending in long and
continuous curves, almost the whole way to
Laguna. The road is excellently made, but
is utterly bare· and uninteresting except for

the views of Santa Cruz lying spread out
below with the blue ocean beyond. When
once the precincts of Laguna are reached,
the road changes in character, and one has
to drive through the town over the most
villainously paved road I have ever seen.
The only comparison I can make, to give
an adequate idea of it, is to compare it with
the log-mended roads of the backwoods of
America, or with the up country stations of
New Zealand, where one has sometimes to
hold on to the seat lest one should be
thrown out of the vehicle, or be bumped to
pieces, as the charioteer cracks his whip
over his team, and dashes along regardless of holes and any impediments of that
nature. Laguna was the ancient capital
of the island, and now possesses a good
English hotel. It is a pleasant and favourite
place to live in during the summer and
autumn months, and indeed, no great heat
is experienced throughout the entire summer ; so that it forms a very convenient
resort for those invalids who cannot or dare
not return to England during that season.
Many of the residents in Orotava and Santa

Cruz go there with their families in May
and remain till October or November, during which period Dr. Victor Perez, of
Orotava, informs me the weather is most
pleasant. It is, indeed, probably the best
of all the higher summer stations, hitherto
available for invalids either in the Canary
Islands or Madeira, and some seem to have
obtained benefit from a stay there. It
seems quite unfit, however, for invalids
during the winter and spring, on account
of its dampness—it occupies the site of an
ancient lake—and the frequency with which
it is visited by cold mists and chilly damp
winds. Mists come down and envelop
Laguna on an average of forty-four days
during the year. The mean temperature
according to observations taken there by
Dr. Perez in 1882, is 63° F., or about six
degrees colder than the Puerto Orotava.
February is the coldest month, with a mean
of 54.8° F.; and August the hottest, with
a mean of 72·2° F. Many delicate persons
find the long drive from Santa Cruz to
Puerto Orotava very trying, not only from
its tediousness and the shaking that has

to be endured in passing through Laguna, but also on account of the chilly winds and mists or rain frequently experienced during the winter months at that elevation, and which form a great contrast to the weather left behind an hour or two before at Santa Cruz. It is very injudicious, therefore, for persons to throw aside their wraps and put on light under-clothing, as they are so apt to do on arriving at Santa Cruz; for many cases of serious chill and illness have thus been caused amongst visitors coming to Orotava.

I found that the Grand Hotel at Orotava, which has been so highly praised, and in some respects over-praised I am afraid, could only entertain about five and twenty guests; so on arriving I found, like the vast majority of visitors, I was placed in one of the more or less unhygienic dependencies,* situated in the centre of the town,

---

* But as the dry-earth system has been adopted in the hotels, a great source of danger in imperfect drains is avoided, and Orotava has so far been entirely free from typhoid fever, which is no slight recommendation.

and devoid of gardens, &c., which make so
much difference in the value and pleasant-
ness of a place for invalids.   One soon
found, however, that Orotava had many
advantages over Las Palmas, even in its
present condition; and not only so, but
that its possibilities also were much greater.
To begin with, the town is far smaller, and
within a very few minutes' walk of any part,
there is a fine sea beach bounded by a nice
level road, which could easily be made into
a good promenade.   Again, though the
town is placed on a low peninsula of land
and but little raised above the sea level, the
ground rises very rapidly, almost precipi-
tately at the back of the town, to a sloping
plateau, with an elevation of about 350 feet,
thus affording splendid sites for the future
building of villas.   There the new Hotel
Company have already commenced to build
a fine hotel, which, it is hoped, will obviate
many of the disadvantages of position,
arrangement and management so much
complained of by many visitors, hitherto,
at the hotels in the town.

There are two places called Orotava:

one, the Puerto or port by the sea, is more
especially the new health resort; while the
other, the Villa, is situated nearly three
miles away, at an elevation of 1200 feet,
and was anciently far the more aristocratic
and important place of the two. The latter
cannot be recommended as a residence for
invalids, as it is situated on a very steep
slope, so that there is not a level walk in
the place; and it is rendered very damp
and depressing by the lowness of the clouds
which often descend the mountain side
above the town, to within a few hundred
feet. For a month or more during my
stay there, I scarcely had a glimpse of sun,
on account of the constant heavy and dense
canopy of clouds overhead, not by any
means the " parasol of fleecy clouds," as it
is sometimes described! The sun would
sometimes shine from six to seven o'clock
in the morning, when it first rose over the
mountains to the east of the valley, then
the clouds would settle down, and nothing
more would be seen of it for the rest of the
day; and this was in the months of April
and May. Such a damp and depressing

climate is not good for an invalid. It is, however, much freer from cloud during the autumn months. This heavy canopy of clouds is not felt so depressing at Puerto Orotava, as it is not so close under the mountains; still, a great deal of sunshine is intercepted, so that during the season 1888-1889, for instance, Mr. Boreham, who kindly supplied me with the results of his observations, found there were only 114¼ hours of bright sunshine in November, 100 in December, 107 in January, 147¾ in February, 149 in March, and 128 in April, as registered by a Jordan's Sun Recorder.

Of the Puerto, Mrs. Stone writes, " It would not be doing Orotava justice to say that it will shortly be a second Funchal; for it can easily rival, and most certainly surpass, Madeira as a winter residence for invalids; besides having attractions that will induce the healthy to resort thither, and prevent it from ever becoming the melancholy hospital that Funchal is."

It is such vague and indefinite comparisons as the above, made in favour of a place well-known and liked by the writer, which so frequently give wrong impressions of places to the public. With the single exception as regards the climate, that there is a greater rainfall on an average at Funchal than at Orotava, everything, it seems to me, is in favour of the former, as regards the class of invalids which ought to be sent to these climates. Again, I quite fail to see what attractions Orotava has for the healthy which Funchal has not, saving for the presence of the Peak itself, but very few, even of the healthy, ever ascend it ; and, furthermore, not only are the excursions to be made from Funchal far more numerous, but the scenery is undeniably far finer. It is not given to every one to be a pioneer like Mrs. Stone, nor to despise the comforts of the hotels and conveyances, or the kind attentions of the hotel proprietors to the wants and requirements of their guests, whether well or ill, as she appears to do.

Though Orotava is situated on the north side of the island it does not experience the cool North-East trade winds in such force, during the winter months, as Las Palmas ; for the Island of Teneriffe is not then so directly in the track of these winds as that of Grand Canary ; though it has the advantage of experiencing them during the summer, when they exercise a grateful and cooling influence on the climate.

In consequence of the heavy swell which usually prevails on this Northern Coast of the island the spray rises in a thick mist, which can be seen extending all along the coast to a distance of several hundred yards inland and to a height of a hundred feet or more.   This salt-laden air must be constantly inhaled by invalids living near the sea, and many cases may reap considerable benefit from it, as such air is considered by some peculiarly good for certain types of phthisis.

Vegetation is decidedly more prolific than around Las Palmas, a very barren place, though it does not equal in luxuriance that of Funchal ; but there is sufficient to render the country green and pleasant to the eye, and most of the land in the valley of Orotava is well cultivated, and the ground is let at high rents for agricultural purposes. Three and even four crops are obtained off the same ground during the year for which irrigation has to be constantly employed.

Notwithstanding the amount of vegetation, garden vegetables are difficult to procure, as also are cow's milk and butter. The latter is not made for sale, as it was an almost unknown product till the last two years, it consequently has to be imported and is generally quite uneatable. Sometimes we used to order it to be removed from the table before we could sit down to a meal! A public market would be a great boon, as it would cause competition, and improve the supply and quality of various articles of food.

There is one good spring for the supply of drinking water, but it is situated a mile from the town, and yet all potable water has to be brought from it. Care should therefore be taken to ensure its coming from the right source, and also that the small barrels in which it is usually brought are kept clean and left open to the air after being emptied. If the bung is replaced they become musty and render the water next time they are used, almost undrinkable from its mouldy flavour, as was frequently the case when I was there. It is cleaner and more satisfactory, therefore, to use earthenware jars for fetching and keeping the water, such as are used in Grand Canary and Madeira.

Mosquitoes are declared to be entirely absent at Orotava, but visitors did not find this to be the case. They were about as numerous as at Funchal, where it is also often stated they are absent. They are, however, far less numerous than in Las Palmas, where they simply swarm.

There are two good drives from Orotava, viz., that towards Laguna, and that in the opposite direction to a village called Icod, where the good driving road ceases. Many think that the possession of these two excellent roads gives Orotava a great pull over Funchal, where there are no wheeled vehicles whatever. Orotava has also borrowed the hammock and the bullock carro as means of locomotion from Madeira, but in consequence of there being so few of either at present, it is hard to get hold of them when wanted.

The mortality from phthisis is small, though the natives are by no means exempt, the death-rate per 1000 at Orotava for the following years was as follows :—in 1875, 0·94 ; 1876, 0·47 ; 1877, 1·0 ; 1878, 1·62 ; and in 1879, 1·41.

The average mortality from phthisis is given as 1·5 per 1000 in Puerto Orotava, 1 per 1000 in the Villa Orotava, ·65 in Laguna, and 3 in Santa Cruz. The general death-rate varies from about 14 to 22 per 1000.

As far as one can reconcile the varying figures of various observers (Honeggar, Belcastel, Biermann), the annual mean temperature of Orotava seems to be about 69° F., or about three degrees warmer than Funchal.

The mean temperature for the four seasons is as follows :—Winter (December, January, February), 63·3 ; Spring (March, April, May), 66·7 ; Summer (June, July, August), 74·9 ; Autumn (September, October, November), 71·8. The winter temperature is thus 2·4° F. warmer than that of Funchal which is 60·9° F.

The mean annual rainfall is given by Honneggar as 13·4 inches, falling on 52 days.

June, July, August and September are practically rainless months, while February is the wettest month, an average of 2·56 inches falling on six days. Snow rarely falls below 2500 feet, and is not often seen except on the mighty El Teide (the Peak), till January or later, but I have seen it low down on the mountains to about that level even in April. The ground being entirely composed of volcanic scoriæ and rock is very porous and quickly dries after even the heaviest rains.

The relative humidity has been given by Dr. Biermann as 67·4 (for the months of January, February, March, April and May) as the mean of three readings at 7 a.m., 2 p.m., and 9 p.m., which does not show any marked degree of greater dryness over Funchal. Mr. Boreham's careful observations during the season of 1888 to 1889, show a decidedly higher degree of (relative) humidity, viz., 77°, from observations taken at 9 a.m., 3 p.m., and 9 p.m. That such a winter as 1888 to 1889 with a great persistence of cloudy weather and Northerly wind should show such a result does not seem so surprising as might at first sight appear. This is not a dry wind by any means, and in the case of Orotava it blows directly off the sea over the valley; but in Madeira it has to pass over the intervening high range of mountains before it reaches Funchal, whereby it loses much of its moisture, and it then descends on the south side of the island as a comparatively dry wind.

The clouds, as in Madeira, are a prominent feature of the climate, and very specially so of Orotava, for they constantly form a dense canopy overhead from the condensation of the moisture in the trade winds as they become cooled in rising over the high barrier of mountains to the south of Orotava. From the northern aspect of this place the clouds naturally intercept far more sunshine than they would do with a southern aspect, such as Funchal, where during the whole of the season of 1888-1889 (November to April) there were only nine days with less than an hour's sunshine.

The North-East wind is the prevailing one, and is chiefly felt at the sea-level. The sea and land breezes are also plainly felt, the former being reinforced and joined with the trade wind when that is blowing. A very hot, dry and parching wind called here the Levante, exactly corresponding to the "Leste" of Madeira, occasionally blows over the islands from the South or South-East, but as its nature and source were described in the last chapter, I shall not again enter into particulars about it.

My meteorological observations taken at Puerto Orotava, for the season of 1887 to 1888 are given in Table I., by which it will be seen that 50° F. was the lowest temperature recorded ; and that the mean temperature of the five winter months to March was 62·8°, which is almost identical with the mean summer temperature of London, *i.e.*, 62·3° F.

It will be gathered from the observations given in Table II., that the season of 1888 to 1889 at Orotava was particularly cool, sunless and damp in comparison with the records of previous years. The mean tem-

perature of the three winter months was
only 58·7, instead of 63·3. The number

TABLE I.

*Record of Temperature taken at Puerto Orotava during
the winter of* 1887-8.

	Nov.	Dec.	Jan.	Feb.	March.
Mean of month.	65·7	64·6	62·2	60·4	61·5
Mean maximum	71·6	70·2	67·8	66·5	67·5
Mean minimum.	59·8	59·	57·6	54·4	55·6
Mean range	11·8	11·2	10·2	12·1	11·9
Highest maximum. . . .	77·	82·†	74·5	73·	76·†
Lowest minimum	53·	56·	50·	50·	53·
Approximate sunshine, hours‡ . . . . }		180	179½	163	234

Thermometers with full northern exposure. No screen used,
which probably renders the results rather lower than if a
Stevenson's screen had been used.

of rainy days was nine more than at
Funchal, and the rainfall nearly an inch
greater in amount, while the relative humidity was also considerable higher.

It may be seen, therefore, that the

* The observations for November were taken by a friend.

† Hot South-East wind or Levante.

‡ The sunshine was taken by observation only. It probably
does not give at the outside an excess of more than 10 per cent.
of bright sunshine.

TABLE II.

Meteorological Observations taken at San Antonio, Orotava, November 1888 to April 1889. by W. L. Boreham, Esq.

346 FEET ABOVE THE SEA.	NOVEMBER.	DECEMBER.	JANUARY.	FEBRUARY.	MARCH.	APRIL.
Mean temperature of month	64·5	60·5	57·8	58·4	59·3	59·9
Mean maximum	69·8	65·6	62·7	64·2	64·5	64·2
Mean minimum	59·3	55·4	53·	52·7	54·1	55·7
Highest maximum	73·8	69·4	66·5	75·5	69·2	66·5
Lowest minimum	54·9	51·8	51·	50·	49·1	49·6
Maximum in sun	152·8	142·9	154·8	149·3		
Minimum on grass	51·	49·4	47·5	39·9	40·3	41·6
Sunshine, hours*	114·15	99·55	107·5	147·40	148·55	127·55
Total rainfall	·513	3·994	2·203	1·430	1·174	·632
Number of days on which ·01 or more rain fell	8	17	13	10	7	8
Relative { 9 a.m.	73	85	75	71	75	73
Humidity. { 3 p.m.	72	82	73	71	75	70
{ 9 p.m.	80	88	82	80	80	80
Barometer, mean 9 a.m. and 9 p.m.	30·205	30·194	30·265	30·242	30·187	30·253
Barometer, highest	30·39	30·47	30·57	30·55	30·36	30·40
Barometer, lowest	30·09	29·72	29·97	29·55	29·87	30·05

* Hours of bright sunshine recorded by a Jordan's Sun Recorder.

balance of fine weather is not *always* in favour of Orotava over Funchal, though as a rule Orotava seems to have a drier and slightly warmer climate than Funchal, and one of much the same equability.*

The climate seems fitted for very much the same class of cases as that of Madeira, though of course being a new place it is thought by its more enthusiastic partisans that its climate will prove a panacea for almost every complaint. So one finds cases of almost every kind there, neuralgia and sciatica, gout and rheumatism, nervous shock, Bright's disease, African fever, laryngitis, asthma, phthisis in all stages and in all constitutions, cases one would have thought just fitted for the climate of Davos, as well as cases so far gone that they should never have left their homes at all; all expecting to find there what they will find nowhere—a perfect climate.

* SEASON, 1888-1889.

	RAINFALL.	DAYS OF RAIN.
Orotava	9.946 inches ...	63
Funchal	9·05 inches ...	54
Difference in favour of Funchal	·896 inches ...	9

It will be seen that I have not written any fanciful or poetical descriptions of these islands such as are so often written; but I have given the facts concerning them, at all events as they appear to me and to the majority of visitors with whom I came into contact while there and since. I have not unfrequently heard visitors to the Canary Islands say that it takes the first fortnight to unlearn all they have previously heard or read about them, and to disabuse their minds of the exaggerated descriptions of weather and scenery which have been circulated! No one, however, can deny that the islands do possess a great deal of beautiful and grand scenery, and a really good though not perfect climate. Teneriffe especially, has great capabilities as a health resort in its dry and yet equable climate, though it still labours under many disadvantages through its lack of development; these, however, are mostly removable by time, by good management, and by the opening up of a more sheltered, and if possible more elevated resort than Puerto Orotava, on the south side of the island to the west of Santa Cruz.

MENTONE, LOOKING EAST.

CHAPTER VI.

THE WESTERN RIVIERA.

THIS most delightful and popular district possesses not only the most lovely stretch of coast and sea scenery in Europe, but also the most delightful winter climate that can be reached with facility by the inhabitants of Great Britain.

The whole coast line from Hyères to Genoa is now roughly included under the title, and it is studded throughout its entire length with most picturesquely situated villages and towns, many of which are most popular winter health resorts, and great is the rivalry amongst them. In this capacity, namely as Winter Health Resorts, there has been a vast amount of discussion as to their rival merits, and indeed some may think a vast deal of hair-splitting as to whether this place or that is the more exposed to the cold winds, whether this place or that is not half a degree the warmer.

Again, each place is divided for further discussion into a West side and an East side,
a situation near the sea and others more
inland, till the minute differences may appear bewildering and unnecessary. There
is, however, more excuse than at first sight
is apparent for this vast amount of sub-
division ; for it is not unfrequently found
that an invalid of excitable temperament,
who cannot sleep or who shows intolerance
of the climate in other ways, when residing
in the confined space, for example, of the
East Bay of Mentone, yet by a move even to
the West Bay, or to San Remo, is rendered
far more comfortable.

Though the whole of the Riviera possesses a somewhat uncertain climate in
comparison with some which are well within
the reach of invalids, and has consequently
had many detractors of late years, yet if it
is looked upon in its proper sphere, and is
not expected to be what it is *not*, *i.e.*, a
warm and equable climate, it is then found
to be, for many complaints, an extremely
valuable and useful climate. It forms a fair
medium between the extremes of the Alpine

Winter Resorts on the one hand, and of
Madeira and the Canary Islands on the
other. It is as absurd to look upon the
climate, as is often done by the advocates of
the Alpine cure, as being a hot and relaxing
one, as to go to the other extreme and
declare it to be a district of such cold and
trying winds that an invalid can rarely
venture out with safety. The fact is, it is a
fine and moderately dry climate, with a
large proportion of bright sunshine and blue
sky. This bright weather and hot sunshine
is, however, often marred and rendered
treacherous by the cold winds so often experienced there; especially is this the case
when the Mistral blows, which is a bitterly
cold North or North-Westerly wind, really
rendering it unsafe for invalids to go out,
notwithstanding that the sun may be shining brightly. It is of an intensely cold
searching character, and on account of its
dryness and strength, it raises clouds of
dust from the dry roads. The contrast between hot sunshine and chilly shade is a
risk always to be remembered, and has constantly to be insisted upon. Nevertheless,

the contrast is small when compared with that experienced at Davos, where the temperature of the sun's rays is frequently higher than that in the Riviera, while the shade temperature would not unfrequently be 30° to 40° F. lower, though usually the atmosphere would be stiller.

Notwithstanding these drawbacks, a winter residence in almost any of the well known resorts along the Riviera must always prove a most valuable change for a very large class of our invalids ; not only on account of the accessibility, general attractiveness and natural beauty of the district, and avoiding as it does any prolonged sea passage, but also on account of the intrinsic merits of the climate ; its stimulating and invigorating properties, the bright sun and large proportion of fine dry days that may be counted upon, and the general geniality of the climate after that of our northern shores.

This geniality of climate is caused mainly by four factors :—

Firstly, by the protection caused by the high Maritime Alps to the north.

Secondly, by the southern aspect of the various resorts; thus they obtain all the sunshine possible.

Thirdly, by the immediate propinquity of the Mediterranean, the water of which is several degrees warmer than that of the Atlantic.

Fourthly, by the radiation and reflection of heat from the limestone mountains, which is especially noticeable at Mentone.

Though the Riviera is so well protected and so favourably placed, it is well known as a very windy district, and these winds are frequently, whether from the North-West (Mistral), or the North-East and East, very cold during the months of February, March and April. It is said that the North-East wind is tempered there in comparison with its northern congeners by the more southern latitude (Sparks), and it no doubt is so to some extent, but certainly this does not apply to the bitter " Mistral."

There is, indeed, no locality on the continent of Europe which is free from the cold winds of spring, even places on the southern coast of Spain do not escape. Meran in the

Austrian Tyrol is said to be protected from them, but, as I have before mentioned, I-have experienced very high and boisterous, as well as very cold snow-bringing winds there even in April and May. One must travel indeed to the islands of the West, to the Canaries or Madeira, before the East wind loses its terrors for the invalid, and even there the Northerly winds are often felt chilly.

The climate is not so noticeable for the small total amount of rain as for the small number of days on which rain falls, and for the large proportion of bright and sunny days. The rainfall may be estimated as varying from 28 to 32 inches, falling on from 60 to 70 days. The actual rainfall is therefore, about double that of Orotava, and almost identical with that of Madeira ; while the number of days on which rain falls is about one-third more than in the Canaries (47), but slightly less than the average given for Madeira, which is 78. The relative humidity may be taken to be about 73 per cent. (Cannes 73 per cent., Mentone 72·8 per cent.).

The mean annual temperature of the Riviera may be taken, as about 60-61° F. (Cannes 60°, Mentone 61° F.), or about 5 degrees colder than Madeira (65·7°) ; while the winter temperature may be taken as about 51° F. (Cannes 50·4°, Mentone 51·5° F.) or about ten degrees colder than the Madeira winter (61·7°).

Snowstorms not unfrequently occur, and though the snow rarely lies for long on the ground, it has been known to remain for several days at Cannes. Sharp frosts are by no means uncommon, and ice on the pools is not a rare sight.

The accommodation in the Riviera is of course excellent, but considering the high prices charged by the hotel keepers, and how much they live by the presence of invalids, one would have thought that they would have endeavoured a little more to meet their wants, and to pay them a little more attention than they do. But this seems far from their principle, which is to make the invalid pay as much as possible for every little extra, which he has indeed the greatest trouble in obtaining. For in-

stance, if an invalid is living *en pension,*
and from indisposition is unable to partake
of the general meal, yet a glass of milk, or a
little beef tea is charged for extra. A lady
was ordered some chicken broth one day,
at a well known hotel by her doctor, and
lo! and behold, she was charged *twelve*
francs for it! Compare this inattentive and
grasping spirit with the hotels of Madeira.
There, the proprietor or manager comes and
asks if anything extra is wanted—a cup of
beef tea for lunch, or a glass of milk on
going to bed and so forth, and if desired it
is supplied regularly, and without any extra
payment. In most places pensions may be
found, which are generally cheaper than the
hotels, but it is very difficult for strangers
to hear of satisfactory ones where they are
likely to be comfortable. Indeed, many
things tend to make living expensive in
the Riviera, so that it is a mistake for invalids to go there, if in consequence of
straightened means, they have to take
north or inferior rooms; to feel the
constant irritation of having to pay for
extras beyond what they had expected; and

have to forego any constant and adequate medical supervision on account of the fees charged, no arrangement as at Davos ever being made as far as I have heard. But when an invalid arrives in the Riviera, it is most important, for more reasons than one, that he should consult one of the resident English physicians;—firstly, that he should be guided as to the best situation for his particular case, as far as can at first be ascertained, before finally settling on any hotel or Villa;—and, secondly, that the physician may be acquainted with the exact condition of the patient, in order that he may more readily judge of any new phase of the case, if his further aid be necessary during the course of the patient's stay.

Two important questions are not unfrequently asked—" When should an invalid return home, and which are the best places to stay at on the way?" This latter question will greatly depend as to when he leaves his winter quarters, and whether he travels homewards by the French route, or whether he proceeds viâ Genoa and the Italian Lakes. Invalids are, in the first

place, far more likely to err on the side of
starting homewards too early, rather than too
late, in the season. Those who set off on
the first approach of warm weather, perhaps
at the end of March or beginning of April,
only too frequently repent their haste; for
all travelling is at that time of the year a
hazardous proceeding for invalids throughout Central Europe. The treacherousness
and changeability of our English climate
in the spring months, is especially felt after
a long sojourn in the warmer and less
changeable climate of the South of Europe.
The end of May or beginning of June is,
indeed, quite as early as those who have
any decided delicacy of the chest, should
venture upon encountering the vicissitudes
of the English climate. The month of
May will be felt by the majority of invalids
too hot in the Riviera; for there is no
doubt that as a rule, and putting aside
individual cases, phthisical patients bear
cold better than heat; the former braces
them up, and invigorates their flagging
energies, while the latter, in many cases,
causes lassitude and depression. From the

middle to the end of April may, therefore, be considered as the most appropriate time for leaving the coast towns of the Riviera. This brings us to the second question, " Where is the best place to spend the intervening month of May ? " If the Eastern route viâ Genoa be taken, the Italian Lakes afford many sheltered, lovely and suitable stopping places, such as Pallanza, Varese, Cadenabbia, etc. Varese may be particularly recommended ; for the hotel, an old Ducal Palace, is situated on rising ground away from the immediate proximity of the lake, and also out of the town, while it possesses beautiful and extensive grounds of its own. There are also numerous walks and drives in the neighbourhood, and many delightful excursions can be made. Invalids staying in the above hotel are well understood, and receive every attention. The district affords wonderful scope for the botanist. Monte Generoso, near the Lake of Como, which has an elevation of about 5000 feet, near the top of which is a good hotel, is often visited, but as it is very subject to be enveloped in clouds till the season is well advanced, it

should not be visited in May by invalids.
Lucerne is another very good stopping
place for the month of May on the home-
ward journey; or if it be determined to
spend the summer in Switzerland, it is a
good starting point for the Engadine or
elsewhere.

If the route through France be chosen,
Grasse so little removed from the direct
route, and hereafter described, would probably afford as good a resort for April and
May as need be looked for; and few would
find it too hot even towards the end of the
latter month. Again, by branching off the
main route at Lyons, the whole district round
the Lake of Geneva is easily reached, with
its many available places for a stay, such as
Montreux, Vevez, Glyon, etc. Bex is also
a favourite spring station, being well sheltered from the Northerly winds, and it is
said to be decidedly drier than Montreux.

Mosquitoes are a great plague to most new
comers, up till about Christmas time, when
they mostly disappear till April or May.
All the beds are, however, provided with
mosquito curtains, so that with care one's

rest at night need not be disturbed. As to all the so-called preventions against their bites, such as sponging over with a solution of carbolic acid, etc., I cannot say I have found any of them effectual.

Phthisis is the chief disease for which amelioration is sought in this climate, and the results obtained compare very favourably with those at other health resorts. Thus Dr. C. T. Williams gives the following results obtained in the Riviera :—62·5 cent. improved or were cured; 20·39 per per cent. remained the same; 17·11 per cent. became worse; but Dr. Hermann Weber's results are hardly as good, viz :—47·6 per cent. improved ; 17·5 per cent. remained the same ; 34·9 per cent. became worse; and he adds, "nowhere else have we met with the occurrence of so many acute and sub-acute affections as among our patients in this region—the chief cause being bronchitis, pneumonia, pleurisy, laryngitis, etc." This is due no doubt to the cold winds, and the contrast between the hot sun and chilly shade, and should be a warning to all invalids to be careful to carry an extra

wrap for the cold, sunless and narrow
streets of the "old towns" and other chilly
or exposed places.   Sufferers from chronic
bronchitis, especially in those of advancing
years, to whom the fogs and damp cold of
our English winter are so fatal, form
another large contingent of the annual
visitors to this region.   Dr. Henry Bennet
calls it "an invaluable climate for weak,
sickly and strumous children."   Cases of
gout, renal disease, rheumatism and dys-
pepsia, generally benefit by a residence in
the Riviera.

Hyères.

In travelling from West to East along the
coast of Provence, the first of these well
known resorts which is reached after leaving Marseilles, is Hyères, though it can
scarcely be strictly called one of the towns
of the Riviera.

It is a quieter, smaller and less fashionable place than most of them, and situated
about three miles inland instead of immediately on the coast.   Furthermore, it is pro-

tected from the sea breezes by the pine covered ridge of hills (La Colline de L'Ermitage), and by the Islands of Hyères. It is also well protected on the north, but on the other hand, it is extremely exposed to the Mistral; and it is acknowledged by nearly all authorities that it suffers more from this cruel wind than any other resort in the Riviera.

About two miles south-west of the town of Hyères lies the picturesque valley of Costabelle, which, with its two large hotels, English church and several villas, forms quite a little colony of its own. Situated on the south side of the pine covered ridge of the L'Ermitage, above mentioned, these hotels are decidedly warmer, and far better protected from the dreaded Mistral than those in Hyères itself. They are also quieter and more pleasant to stay at, for those who prefer to be out of the noise and dust of the town.

The chief characteristic of Hyères is its distance from the sea, and therefore it is less exposed to sea influence. Consequently the climate is less exciting than some of the

other resorts, and more suitable for those
who cannot stand immediate proximity to
the sea.

CANNES.

Proceeding eastwards, the next resort of
importance met with is the beautiful and
fashionable town of Cannes, which is especially popular with the English.

It is a comparatively scattered town, and
as there are many villas having private
gardens attached to them, it covers a large
space of ground; while the mountains do
not closely encircle it as at Mentone, so that
there is no feeling of confinement, as is
sometimes felt by visitors in the latter place.
This very openness, however, renders it
more subject to be swept by winds, which
are very prevalent, and especially by the
Mistral. On an average there are seven.
days per month of strong winds or gales
throughout the winter, so it must be put
down as a very windy place.

Cannes is situated on the shores of two
bays, an East and a West bay, which are

divided by a high ridge of ground, the Mont Chevalier, on which stands a conspicuous old tower. The chief business part of the town, as well as the harbour, lie to the east of this ridge ; while many of the larger villas stand on more elevated ground to the west. A fine broad promenade runs along the whole length of the East bay, called the Boulevard de la Croisette ; but the pleasure of walking or driving along it is greatly marred by the atrocious smells from the drains, which empty themselves into the sea along its course, and which are not carried out far enough into deep water to obviate this nuisance. This Boulevard terminates at the Cape de la Croisette, exactly opposite which, and at a distance of a mile, and one and a half miles, respectively, are situated the picturesque islands of St. Marguerite and St. Honorat. These islands are well worth visiting for the splendid view of Cannes and the Esterel mountains to be obtained from them ; as well as for the interest attaching to the fort on the former island, and to the old Monastery on the latter.

The drives around Cannes are very

numerous, and are a decided attraction; the aspect of the country allowing of many more than is the case at Mentone or San Remo. The large amount of dust on some of the roads is a decided drawback, especially to those invalids who find dust irritating to their lungs.

Many kinds of sweet scented flowers are grown in large quantities in the neighbourhood for the manufacture of various scents, this industry being carried on very extensively there and at Grasse. It is said that during the month of May 100,000 ℔ of rose petals, 40,000 ℔ of orange flowers, etc., are used daily in the various distilleries.

The hotel accommodation is very extensive, for there are at least eighty large hotels in various positions, so that there is afforded a large choice of situation; not to mention the several hundred villas which are to be let furnished for the season, but at very high prices.

The water supply is considered very good, but as it is brought in a small open canal for thirty miles, it must run a considerable

risk of contamination, and should be efficiently filtered before delivery.

It is to be hoped after the energetic and
public-spirited protest made recently by a
well known Englishman, against the bad
sanitary arrangements of some of the hotels,
and the ready way some of the proprietors
have responded, in adopting the recom-
mendations of the sanitary engineers, that
less will be heard in the future of typhoid
fever, etc. It is a great pity that similar
action cannot be insisted upon in many
other health resorts.

Cannes has for the six winter months
(Nov. to April) a mean temperature of
50·4° F., a mean maximum of 56·9° F., and a
mean minimum of 44° F. ; an average rainfall of 21·80 inches, falling on 58 days ; and
a relative humidity of 73 per cent. Snow
occasionally falls, but it seldom lies on the
level for more than a few hours.

The air is decidedly tonic and bracing,
and consequently scrofulous and anæmic
cases do well; while some persons with
nervous constitutions, or those with a
tendency to fever find the air too exciting.

Of places in the neighbourhood, Le
Cannet situated on rising ground two and a
half miles to the north of Cannes, is decidedly more sheltered from both land and
sea winds than the latter, and thus presents
some advantages to invalids over Cannes
itself.

Grasse

Is situated at an elevation of 1000 feet above
the sea, and about nine miles from Cannes,
inland.   It is much liked by some people,
and presents some advantages over the
coast towns of the Riviera for certain cases,
while it is of course decidedly cooler.   Invalids can therefore stay there with advantage
later than in the towns along the coast.

Dr. Yeo says that in 1887 snow fell on
six days, the minimum temperature fell to
26·6° F., and the mean minimum for the
three winter months (Dec., Jan. and Feb.)
was 35·7° F.

The hotel accommodation at the Grand
hotel is now excellent, and the sanitary arrangements have been carefully attended to.

NICE.

This large and fashionable winter resort of the French possesses many artificial advantages; but, at the same time, it also possesses most of the drawbacks of the Riviera for the invalid, in a concentrated degree.

In the first place, being a large and fashionable town, pleasure and gaiety are considered before health; secondly, it is greatly exposed to cold winds, which are frequently high and strong; and thirdly, it is extremely dusty. It, however, possesses a dry, sunny and bracing climate, and is found to be very invigorating for those classes of invalids, such as dyspeptics, and those who are suffering from anæmia and general debility, who are not affected by the foregoing drawbacks.

During the winter season, from Oct. 1st to May 31st, there are on an average, 135·8 sunny days, 53·3 cloudy, and 52·8 rainy. The mean winter temperature is 50·9; almost identical with that of Cannes.

The magnificent " Promenade des An-
glais," said to be one of the finest in
Europe, and a mile and a half long, affords
a splendid open and level walk for invalids,
though it is frequently found to be very
windy.   This promenade was so named,
because it was constructed at the expense
of the British residents at Nice, about sixty
years ago, to give employment to the poor.

Cimiez, a suburb two miles to the north
of Nice, is situated on elevated ground, and
is said by some to be more protected from
the cold winds than Nice.   But Dr. Sparks
doubts this, and declares, " The chief advantage of Cimiez is its distance from the
sea, and from the whirl and dust of a great
and fashionable town."

Monte Carlo.

This lovely spot, one of the prettiest on
the whole line of coast, has advantages for
the invalid in its very protected position,
and it is said to possess an even warmer
climate than Mentone ; but it is rendered
unpleasant to many by the class of people

drawn there by the too well known gaming tables. Thus it is comparatively neglected at present by invalids. From the close proximity of the mountains to the sea, the walks and drives in the neighbourhood are necessarily limited in number, and those few are hilly.

The picturesque old town of Monaco is built on a rocky promontory with precipitous cliffs between one and two hundred feet high, and as it bends towards the south-east it forms the little bay of Monaco which possesses an excellent beach for bathing.

MENTONE,

The next place we have to mention, has become with English invalids, though it is probably not so with those in health, the most popular of the Riviera resorts. It is situated like Cannes on the shores of two bays, an Eastern and a Western, the former being the smaller, the warmer and the most sheltered from winds. These two subsidiary bays, as we may call them, form the large indentation of the coast, bounded by Cape St. Martin on the west, and Cape Mortola on the east. As at Cannes the two bays are divided by a ridge of hills, which runs southwards to the sea from the grand range of mountains to the north, which forms the amphitheatre in which Mentone lies. On this ridge the old town of Mentone is built; while the new town stretches along the shores of the bays to the east and to the west of it. The great beauty of the district is well seen from the road to Roquebrunnen, as it crosses the ridge of hills which encloses the district of Mentone on the west, and which runs southwards from the main range of mountains to form the promontory of Cape St. Martin. From there also a splendid view of Mentone is obtained, and its wonderfully sheltered position more fully realised. Viewing this lovely place from these points, one cannot be surprised at the rapturous expressions of admiration one often hears of this far-famed spot.

The drives and excursions in the neighbourhood are more numerous than at the

other resorts on the Riviera, excepting
Cannes; Cape St. Martin is always a resource, and besides the Corniche road, the
Gorbio, the Borrigo and the Turin valleys,
as well as the road to Castellar, all afford
pleasant drives and excursions.

Hotels are good and numerous in both
bays, and afford plenty of variety in situation; while some are a considerable way
from the sea, others are so close to it that
the ceaseless noise of the waves on the
shingle, especially in rough weather, is felt
to be an annoyance by some invalids.

Though I do not possess any extensive
personal acquaintance with the climate of
Mentone, yet from all accounts and from
my own enjoyment of the climate when
there, one quite feels that Dr. Henry
Bennet's eulogisms of the climate are
quite justified. The air is fresh, tonic and
bracing, and is rarely too keen, as it is so
greatly protected from the cold winds so
generally complained of in the Riviera;
while the Mistral, though occasionally felt,
is a comparatively rare wind.

The mean temperature of the six winter

months, from November to April, is slightly
higher than Cannes, and is given as 51·5° F. ;
the lowest minimum of the winter is rarely
as low as in many other places along the
coast ; this accounts, no doubt, for the suc-
cess which the cultivation of the lemon
meets with, for the lemon groves are quite
a feature of the district.   Though this
demonstrates great mildness of climate, yet
it does not prove absence of frost, for the
lemon tree can stand 7° F. or 8° F. of dry
frost without being injured.   Every fifteen
or twenty years, however, comes a frost
which works terrible havoc amongst the
trees, and causes great loss to the culti-
vators.   The orange can stand two or three
degrees more frost than the lemon, and is
altogether a hardier tree.

The rainfall is given as 16·88 inches for
the six winter months, falling on 47 days,
and the relative humidity is 72·8 per cent.

The East bay of Mentone is probably the
most sheltered nook along the whole coast,
and is therefore particularly fitted for those
patients who are unusually sensitive to cold
winds ; for these are during the spring

months quite a characteristic of the Northern Mediterranean littoral, and often give
such patients attacks of pleurisy and bronchial catarrhs. Other patients, however,
who are not so sensitive and who require a
more bracing atmosphere find the confined
space of the East bay oppressive and depressing, and for them the West bay is
much more suitable.

BORDIGHERA.

After crossing the Italian frontier at
Ventimiglia, we next come upon Bordighera, which consists as usual of an old and
a new town.

It differs from all the other resorts on this
coast, in being situated on a promontory
instead of in a bay. Perhaps it is for this
reason that it is the least strikingly beautiful
of them all.

The old town " consists of houses closely
packed together on an eminence, to the east
of what may be called the plain of Bordighera. It has the usual narrow streets,
rather smelly, not overclean, here and there

arched over, or else buttressed across so as to weld all the houses more or less into one mass."

From the high ground immediately below the old town, a very extensive line of sea coast can be seen in either direction; although the view westwards extending as far as the Esterel mountains beyond Cannes is far more striking than the view eastwards, which only extends as far as Cape Verde, the eastern boundary of the bay of San Remo.

The modern part of Bordighera lies on a flat piece of ground to the West of the old town, and very little raised above the sea level. The main road runs along this flat plain and close to the sea, separated, however, from it by the railway and a few scattered houses. Building has taken place to a considerable extent along this exposed and dusty road, and indeed the two principal hotels are situated close upon it.

It would have been far better both for shelter and for sanitary reasons, for the villas and hotels to have been built a little further inland, where the ground begins to rise towards the hills, and along the base of which runs the old Roman road, now made into an excellent carriage road, and affording excellent sheltered sites for villas. Between the two above-mentioned main roads lie most of the modern villas, ensconced amongst the olive woods, and though the ground is very flat on which they are situated, from its geological nature it is exceedingly porous, and thus affords good drainage and prevents any stagnation of surface water.

In considering the climate as it affects invalids, it is important to remember that instead of being placed in a protected bay, or two or three miles inland as is Hyères, Bordighera is situated on a promontory, and is therefore much more exposed to sea influence.

Sea winds are therefore the prevailing ones, and the East wind and not the Mistral, is the coldest and most felt. It is undoubtedly a windy place, and in the exposed parts winds are much felt, but level and protected walks are to be found amongst the olive woods, and up the valleys inland, which is a great advantage to invalids. The mean winter temperature is very much the same as that of Mentone, being given as 51·3. The climate is tonic and bracing, and is specially fitted for cases of a scrofulous nature and is markedly suitable for children.

SAN REMO.

San Remo, only four miles further eastwards, has rapidly grown in popularity as a health resort during the last few years ; and its having been chosen by the medical advisers of the late Emperor Frederick, as a suitable residence for him during his last illness, has further drawn attention to it.

It is situated in a bay and is well protected behind by an amphitheatre of mountains, rising to a height of 4,000 feet in Monte Bignone, and terminating in Cape Verde on the east, and Cape Nero on the west of the bay. The town consists as usual of an old and new part, the former rises very picturesquely up the rather steep sides of a spur of the mountains, and is crowned at the top by a large domed Church—the Sanctuary.

The streets of the old town are very narrow and dark, the houses high and united to the opposite ones by numerous arched buttresses, to guard against earthquakes, which seemingly must have been far more frequent in former times than of late years; the assumed security of this whole district, however, was rudely shaken by the sad and destructive earthquake of February, 1887, which disastrously proved its liability to them.

The picturesque streets of these old towns are much frequented by artists, who are often to be seen with their easels, encamped in the centre of one of these dirty streets, seemingly quite oblivious to their insanitary and odorous surroundings! If they are invalids they should sacrifice their artistic tastes out of respect for their health, and avoid these favourite haunts, in favour of the many lovely spots to be found with nature's purest surroundings.

The modern part of San Remo stretches along the bay, nearly to an equal extent

westwards and eastwards of the old town ;
and the hotels are about equally divided on
either side, the English generally preferring
those on the west side.

The accommodation the hotels afford is
good, but they are generally considered
very expensive, which is especially felt by
invalids, as all extras are charged for very
highly in addition to the "pension" prices.

The climate of San Remo is said to be
one of the mildest on the Riviera ; its most
marked features are, its greater degree of
dryness, and its greater equability. The
mean winter temperature for the six winter
months, from November to April, is 51·3°
F., which is almost identical with that
given for Bordighera and Mentone. Sharp
frosts occasionally occur, and Dr. Sparks
speaks of seeing ice an inch thick in
January, 1869. The annual rainfall is given
as 28·78 inches, but these statistics are not
very reliable. From October to April it is
said there are, on an average, only 35 days
on which rain falls. The Mistral occasionally blows, but the winds which are most
acutely felt are the easterly ones, the North-

East or " Grecco " sometimes being a very cold wind. The climate is rather less bracing and stimulating than most of the places before mentioned along this coast, and its greater equability and soothing nature is best suited for those of a nervons, irritable and sensitive constitution.

ALASSIO.

The last of the well known resorts along the Western Riviera before reaching places, such as Pegli, which are really suburbs of Genoa, is the small and unpretending town of Alassio. It differs from the other places we have mentioned in having a summer as well as a winter season, as it is frequented by the English during the winter, and by the Italians during the summer. The latter go there in large numbers to avail themselves of the excellent sea bathing ; the firm sand of the shore affording an excellent beach both for bathing and walking. A non-pebbly shore is not to be met with in any place that we have mentioned along this

coast, and therefore forms a delightful
variety and gives a further attraction to this
place.

The town consists of a long straggling
street, running parallel to, and placed
almost upon, the shore ; most aggravatingly
shutting out all view of the sea, and leaving
scarcely any approaches to the sea beach.
A few villas belonging to English residents
are scattered about, chiefly along the
Albenga Road, beyond the old town to the
east, and also upon the slopes of the hills
which rise at the back of the town, and
where also the pretty little English Church
is situated.

The hotel accommodation is decidedly
poor, the Grand Hotel situated right on
the beach is perhaps the best, though the
proximity to the sea on the one hand, and
to the old town on the other, are certainly
drawbacks to its position.

Alassio does not pretend to vie with the
larger and more fashionable stations of the
Riviera, nor does there seem much enter-
prise amongst the natives to induce invalids
to visit it; and its having suffered so

severely from the late earthquake will probably further retard its development.

There are no reliable statistics as to the
climate, but it probably does not afford so
warm a winter resort as Mentone or San
Remo. It certainly seems cooler in the
latter part of the spring, for visitors are not
unfrequently recommended to break their
journey there, and are able to remain later
than elsewhere along this coast.

CHAPTER VII.

Miscellaneous Resorts.

I PROPOSE, in this the last chapter, to give some brief notes on various resorts in different parts of the world, which I have visited from time to time, chiefly when in health. Though my stay at many of these places was short, some invalids may find these notes of use and interest, and others who are contemplating a voyage to the Antipodes may be glad to learn something of the climate that awaits them.

With regard to European resorts, I shall only further mention Arcachon, Biarritz, Pau and the neighbouring Pyrenean resorts; also Meran. Algiers, as being so popular and well known,* has also been included.

One of our own favourite English Sanatoria on the South Coast, may be here men-

---

* A few places which I have not visited, *e.g.,* Algiers have been included for the sake of completeness.

GENERAL VIEW OF MERAN.—TYROL.

tioned for the purpose of comparison with
the many foreign resorts which have been
referred to; and perhaps Bournemouth is
as suitable a place as can be chosen, for if
it is scarcely as warm as some stations,
still it has the advantage over them of
being drier and more sunny.

The indiscriminate writing up of Foreign
Sanatoria has certainly done much harm,
and has been the cause of great disappoint-
ment not only to physicians at home, but
also to their patients. It is not surprising
that a reaction is taking place in favour of
our home stations, and that many are beginning to think that there is but little to be
gained by going abroad, and encountering
all the expense and inconvenience which
that entails. This opinion undoubtedly
holds good for large classes of patients who
are now sent abroad ; but there is, certainly,
one class of disease *i.e.*, all chest complaints,
which can in the majority of cases be more
effectually treated by a judiciously chosen
residence abroad than at home. Of this
fact all who have any extended experience
of foreign climates can scarcely have any

reasonable doubt, notwithstanding the oft-
quoted drawbacks to a foreign residence, the
reality of which no one wishes to deny; and
it would be a great mistake if many who are
able to leave England during the winter
were not advised to do so. Though fully
convinced of this, one does not wish to deny
for a moment the great value of such resorts
as Bournemouth, Torquay, Ventnor, etc.,
when compared with our cold, damp, sunless
and foggy inland towns, for those invalids
who cannot afford to go abroad, or who
cannot be persuaded to leave their own
country and friends.

Even at these well known South Coast
stations, how frequently during the winter,
and especially during the spring months,
are large numbers of phthisical invalids
unable to get out for days, nay, even weeks
together, though fresh air is all essential
to them. Whereas, in such climates as
Mentone or Madeira, they would rarely be
kept to the house for more than a day or
two at a time, and that only occasionally.

It is the same with the large class of
patients who suffer from yearly recurring

attacks of bronchitis. Indeed, one may safely say, that a delicate invalid would be kept indoors less during any winter month in such climates, than during the average English summer. Unfortunately, many leave England with the idea that they will find a perfect climate in the foreign country to which they are going, and of which no doubt they have heard nothing but praise. Consequently they are disappointed in not finding the Elysium they expected, and perhaps were led to expect, for they then find that there are certain drawbacks which every place must have of one kind or another; for a perfect place with perfect surroundings and climate will never be found.

Many, however, rashly rush abroad to places which are not sufficiently developed, but which may have been much advertised, or recommended by robust persons travelling for pleasure, who have really no experience of the requirements of the delicate.

When, for example, a man whose name is known throughout Europe (but not a physician) gravely recommends consump-

tives to take up their abode on the " Peak
of Teneriffe above the clouds," simply because the climate is dry, utterly regardless
of any other consideration, it is not surprising that many rash experiments of foreign places are made, and that many do
return home unimproved in health and disappointed with the results of their residence
abroad.

BOURNEMOUTH.

Bournemouth has very rapidly grown
from a small fishing village, to be one of
the most popular of our seaside resorts,
not only for invalids, but also for those who
wish to spend a pleasant holiday at the
seaside.

It is only five and twenty years ago,
since the author remembers having to coach
from Holmsley Station, twelve miles distant, then the nearest point of railway.
Bournemouth then consisted of only about
four hundred houses, and a population of
three thousand ; whereas now its population amounts to thirty-two thousand. Many

who knew it in its earlier days, cannot help feeling that it is overbuilt, and some of its charm therefore departed ; it, nevertheless, still possesses to some extent its special characteristics, and on all sides may be seen the remnants of the old pine woods, for which it is so noted, bordering the roads or surrounding and sheltering the many scattered villas, and giving off their pleasant balsamic and healthy odours.

Bournemouth is situated in a wide and open bay, formed and protected on the West by the Isle of Purbeck, and on the East by Hengistbury Head and the Isle of Wight, whilst it is fully open to the South. It is divided by the valley of the little river Bourne into an eastern and a western portion ; this valley is occupied by the pleasure grounds which now extend from the shore for a mile inland, and are prettily laid out, and possess many level and sheltered paths for invalids. The ground rises gradually on each side of the valley to about 140 feet, and on this elevated position most of the villas and private residences are situated, extending now along the cliffs East

P

and West for a great distance. There are
numerous level walks on the cliffs, well
provided with seats; during the hottest
season of the year a pleasant sea breeze
may usually be found there, while the pine
woods close at hand, especially on the East
cliff, yield sheltered walks in windy weather.
Besides many walks and drives, Bournemouth also possesses a fine pier, an excellent sandy beach for bathing and for children to play upon, with a tide which only
ebbs and flows a few feet, and an excellent
service of pleasure steamers. Altogether,
Bournemouth has many natural attractions,
which have been well supplemented by good
drainage, a good water supply, and other
sanitary advantages.

The climate of Bournemouth is intermediate in character between the relaxing and
the bracing English seaside resorts, such
as Torquay, Llandudno, and the Channel
Islands on the one hand, and Eastbourne,
Hastings, and Margate on the other. The
mean annual temperature is 49·9° F.; the
mean winter temperature from November
to April 43·3° F.; and that of the three

coldest months, December, January, February, 41·6° F. The mean temperature, therefore, for the six winter months is about 8° F. cooler than the Riviera, 18° F. cooler than Madeira, and 2° F. cooler than Pau; while the mean of the three coldest months is almost identical with that of Pau, and slightly higher than that of Biarritz. The amount of sunshine is very good, but is slightly less than that of Ventnor or East-bourne; the average for the past ten years is 1570 hours per annum.

The annual rainfall is 31 inches, falling on 140 days, against 30·21 inches at Hastings; 23·7 inches at Kew; and 23·7 inches at Margate. The number of rainy days is decidedly less than at some other English resorts (Torquay 180 to 200), but it is more than double the number experienced in the Riviera. The relative humidity is said to range between 75 and 86 per cent. The climate is therefore fairly dry, but it cannot very well maintain the claim made for it, " that it is the driest place in the United Kingdom," nor that " its climate is peculiarly beneficial to those invalids who find

the *moist* climate of the Riviera debilitating ! ''

As might have been expected, Westerly
and South-Westerly winds are the prevailing ones, but East and North-East winds
are often unpleasantly felt in the spring,
and in some seasons are very persistent ;
sea mists are also occasionally experienced.

Bournemouth, indeed, has excellent re-
commendations for the invalid in its sheltered position, its moderately dry and
equable climate, its dry and sandy subsoil,
its good accommodation, and in its many
natural and artificial attractions before
mentioned.

The Mont Dore establishment has a very
complete set of baths of every description
attached to it, namely, Turkish, sea-water,
shower, vapour, needle and douche, etc.,
besides possessing special chambers for
carrying out the inhalation, spray and
vapour treatments of the throat, etc. Massage treatment is also practised.

The results obtained in the treatment
of phthisis are fairly satisfactory, both in
the Sanatorium and amongst private pa-

tients ; Dr. C. J. and C. T. Williams record
improvement in 65 per cent. of their cases,
10 per cent. remained stationary, and 25
per cent. became worse. It is also a peculiarly useful climate for delicate, scrofulous,
or rachitic children, and for catarrhal laryngitis, asthma, and convalescence from acute
diseases.

ARCACHON.

Let us now pass from the English
Bournemouth to what has been termed
the Bournemouth of France, viz., Arcachon. This resort, like the favourite
English one, has been built amongst the
pine woods, which cover the once bare sand
hills that separate the plains of Les Landes
from the Atlantic Ocean. Situated on these
pine covered sand hills surrounding an extensive salt water lake, which only com-
municates with the sea by a narrow channel
about a mile wide, it affords an excellent
sheltered spring and autumn, rather than a
winter residence for invalids ; for it is said
that the accommodation is not adapted to

the requirements of English invalids during the winter, and that then it has a deserted and "triste" appearance. It is much more sheltered than Biarritz from the Westerly gales, and during the winter the temperature rarely falls below freezing.

The climate is softer and more soothing, but less tonic and bracing than that of the Riviera ; and it is therefore more adapted to inflammatory conditions. Whether due to the sea influences, the dry sandy subsoil, or the balsamic exhalations of the pine forest, seems uncertain, but many invalids do obtain decided benefit from a stay at Arcachon.

BIARRITZ.

This is a popular and fashionable bathing place and summer resort with the French and Spanish. It is much more exposed than Arcachon to Atlantic storms, and in winter "is subject to frequent and sudden changes of temperature." It seems, on the whole, but little better as a winter and spring residence than some of our own

English Southern health resorts. The mean temperature for the first four months of the year is both more equable and higher at Bournemouth than at Biarritz; at the former the mean is 43·4° F., while at Biarritz it is only 41·9° F.

If an invalid has to be expatriated, and undergo all the fatigues and inconveniences of a long journey, and the discomforts of a residence in a foreign land, it should at all events be, if possible, to a place which is appreciably better than can be found in his own country. Biarritz seems more suitable as a residence for those who simply require change of air, and for certain classes of nervous and dyspeptic persons, than for those suffering from chest complaints.

PAU.

Pau is in the province of the Basses Pyrenees, and is very prettily situated on high ground overlooking the valley of the Gave ; from some parts of the town, such as the Place Royal, a fine and extensive but distant view of the Pyrenees can be obtained.

It was formerly a very popular winter resort for invalids, and has been much lauded as such, but with the opening up of the Riviera, Algiers, Egypt, &c., which are now made so accessible, it has quite gone out of favour as a suitable residence for chest cases, its climate being now acknowledged to be greatly inferior to many others. Dr. More Madden speaks of it as being "essentially cold, variable, damp and dreary during the winter months." The mean annual temperature is 56·1° F; the mean winter temperature 41·8° F., or almost identical with that of Bournemouth (41·6° F.); the mean spring temperature is 54° F., and the mean for the six winter months from November to April, 45·7°, or only 2° F. warmer than Bournemouth, and 5° F. colder than the Riviera. The thermometer often falls below freezing, on an average of twenty-five nights during the winter, and snow falls on eleven days. The rainfall during the winter months is 26·87 inches, falling on 69 days, and during the year 42 inches on 119 days;

also, the relative humidity is very high. There is a remarkable freedom from wind, but as a consequence fogs are not at all unfrequent.

The damp, cold, and variable climate, renders it an unfit winter residence for cases of phthisis and for most cases of bronchitis. Some cases of asthma are said to do very well.

There are many very lovely and pleasant resorts amongst the Pyrenees, which can be visited in spring and summer from Pau, if those who have wintered there, or in Malaga, Algiers, etc., do not intend returning home during the summer. Most of these places are, however, rather enervating, and though situated at considerable elevations they do not possess the stimulating and invigorating air which is experienced amongst the Swiss mountains; yet as very many phthisical persons resort to them for the sake of taking the waters, which are said to do so much good in certain cases, a few of the best known places may here be mentioned.

Eaux Bonnes, one of the best known of these resorts to English physicians, can now be easily reached by rail from Pau; Laruns, the terminus of the branch of the railway which runs up the Vallée d'Ossau, being only about three miles distant. It is picturesquely situated at the mouth of a gorge, and is thus surrounded on all sides by mountains, excepting on that by which it is approached from Laruns. The rocky sides of the narrow platform on which the town is built, have actually had to be blasted away to make room for building. Notwithstanding that it appears so shut in, there are several very pleasant walks to be had amongst the woods on the mountain sides, and which have been formed at great expense; the chief of these is called the Promenade Horizontale, a capital, level, and well made road, running along the side of the mountain towards Eaux Chaudes, and commanding beautiful and extensive views of the Vallée d'Ossau.

Eaux Bonnes, as is the case with most of these Pyrenean resorts, is very popular with the French and Spanish, but is very little frequented by the English, either for health or pleasure.

The sulphur waters are used both locally (for gargling and inhalation) and internally, and are considered by French physicians to have a remarkable curative effect in phthisis, many regarding them as almost a specific in that disease. This opinion is not held by English physicians, though the beneficial effects of the waters in certain local manifestations of that disease, such as tubercular laryngitis, are recognised, as well as in other less serious forms of throat disease, such as is commonly called clergyman's sore throat, and in chronic catarrhal affections. When I was there in the month of June, the climate seemed scarcely appropriate for phthisical patients, for it was damp, warm and enervating, with thick fogs enveloping the whole town every morning, which used not to lift till midday.

Eaux Chaudes is very beautifully situated on the banks of Gave, in the midst of moun-

tains, the sides of which are clothed to
their very summits with chestnut, box, and
pine trees. It is about an hour's drive from
Eaux Bonnes, the latter half of which is up
a grand and narrow gorge through which
the Gave rushes, often several hundred feet
below the level of the road. This gorge
suddenly opens out, and the village of Eaux
Chaudes then appears in the wider valley
which is then entered upon. It is not a
popular resort at present, and its sulphur
waters and baths seem to a great extent
deserted.

CAUTERETS.

Cauterets is reached after a pretty drive
of about seven miles up a picturesque valley
from the railway at Pierrefitte. The valley
then seems to end in a "cul de sac," formed
by high mountains and in which Cauterets
lies embosomed. Out of this "cul de sac,"
however, several mountain valleys lead to
picturesque and interesting spots, the most
noted of which is the Pont d'Espagne, and
the wild and beautiful Lac de Gaube.

Cauterets is situated at an elevation of 3,050 feet, but being so enclosed by mountains, it possesses rather a hot and oppressive summer climate. This is the more felt from the hotels being situated in the close streets of the town. In fact this is one of the drawbacks felt throughout the whole of the Pyrenees, that there are no hotels placed in pleasant and airy situations, as in Switzerland; but in all the resorts the hotels are all crowded into the streets of the various towns.

The bathing establishments are very complete, and Cauterets is looked upon as a real health, rather than a pleasure, resort by the visitors who follow up the treatment with assiduity and regularity. Crowds of patients may be seen at 7 a.m. daily, going to and returning from the various springs, each with their small graduated glass in a little netted bag slung from their fingers, parasol, or coat buttons. The springs are all highly charged with sulphuretted hydrogen gas, and vary in temperature from 55° F. to 145° F. They are very useful in some skin diseases, chronic rheumatism,

and as at Eaux Bonnes, in throat affections ; and, according to the French physicians, in phthisis.

St. Sauveur is quite a small place on the
road to the village and far-famed Cirque de
Gavarnie, one of the chief points of interest
for the tourist in the Pyrenees.   St. Sauveur
itself possesses some similar springs to the
other Pyrenean Spas, only they are weaker.
The residence of the late Emperor Napoleon
III. and the Empress Eugenie, much increased its popularity.

BAGNÈRES DE LUCHON.

Luchon is the gayest and most popular
of the Pyrenean health resorts, and is quite
a fashionable resort of the Parisian, remind-
ing one, with their gay costumes, of Trouville
in the summer or of Nice in the winter.   Indeed, pleasure and the desire to forget the
ills to which flesh is heir to, seem to take
the first place in the consideration of the
visitors, instead of the serious business of
drinking the waters and taking the baths

which pervades most of the other bathing establishments, although this object, in reality, has brought most of the visitors together to this lovely spot.

The hotel accommodation is of course very good, but rather expensive during the height of the season. The public gardens are most pleasant, the walks formed through the woods are most delightful to wander along on hot days, and there are numerous excursions in the neighbourhood for the stronger class of patients.

The "Etablissement Thermal" is very complete, and provision is made for the application of the waters in every conceivable manner, by inhalation, pulverisation, douches, etc. ; it also possesses numerous single baths, and several swimming baths.

There are many springs of various temperatures containing sulphuretted hydrogen and the sulphides in various degrees of strength. The treatment of disease by these waters is very extended, for they are used in chronic rheumatism, various skin diseases, in the earlier stages of phthisis, and "for the relief of chronic chest affec-

tions, as bronchitis, laryngitis, and all catarrhal conditions of the air passages."

Notwithstanding the great belief in the
efficacy of these sulphur springs amongst
the French physicians as before stated, and
which is also held by English physicians for
some affections, yet there is a large body
of medical opinion which assigns the whole
benefit attained at such waters simply to
the effects of the hot water bathing, the
drinking of large quantities of hot water,
to the inhalation of moist warm air, to the
increased amount of exercise in the open
air, to the climate, and to the regulated
diet and hygienic rules enforced by the
physicians on their patients at such resorts,
rather than to any special efficacy of the
sulphur waters themselves.   Even a German doctor, who may be supposed to be
much in favour of bathing establishments,
writes in Von Ziemssen's " Handbook of
General Therapeutics : " " Many of the
procedures, carried on at such baths belong
to the large chapter of blind experiment
and of speculation, and have gone so far,
that when we send patients to certain baths

we are obliged to give them letters warning
them against some extravagant and sense-
less proceedings, which are nevertheless
popular."

MERAN.

The only other European resort that I
shall here allude to is Meran in the Austrian
Tyrol, which is, amongst English physicians, certainly growing in popularity as
a winter health resort for phthisical patients, though it has been known and duly
appreciated by the Austrians, especially by
the Viennese, for a long time past.

Meran is beautifully situated on the
southern side of the Tyrolese mountains, at
an elevation of about a thousand feet above
the sea, and surrounded on every side
except towards the South by an amphitheatre of mountains rising to a height of
from 9,000 to 10,000 feet. These mountains form a great protection to Meran and
its suburbs of Obermais and Untermais;
but this protection is not complete, for there
are two gaps in them, one to the N.E., and

the other to the N.W., through which the
Passer and Adige flow to mingle their
waters about a mile below the town of
Meran. In stormy weather and especially
in the spring months when Northerly winds
are most prevalent, cold blasts sweep down
these branch valleys upon Meran, and are
much felt. The spring, too, being remarkably dry, the dust at that season is very
trying, and as I have before said in Chapter
III., such dense clouds of it frequently pass
down the valley as to completely blot out
the landscape, and I have myself been kept
to the house for three days together by the
violence of the wind, and the quantities of
dust driven along by it, penetrating every-
where.

The old town of Meran is interesting to
the tourist, but undoubtedly the best quarter
for invalids is Obermais, which is considerably elevated above the level of the valley.
It thus escapes any dampness and fog
which may exist in the flat valley, during
the rainy months of October, November,
and December, while also, to a great extent, it escapes the cold blasts of wind

above mentioned. The lower districts have, however, easier access to the splendid level promenade and gardens along the banks of the Passer. About the centre of the promenade the Kurhaus is placed, where hydropathic, compressed air, massage, and other treatments are carried out, and opposite to which the band plays daily.

Meran has decidedly a cold winter, skating often being possible for nearly the whole of the months of December and January. The winter, however, is a short one, there being a very sudden fall of temperature from the mean of October to that of November, namely from 55° F. to 42° F., and a correspondingly sharp rise from March to April, namely from 46° F. to 54° F.

January is the coldest month, the mean temperature being 32·6° F. The mean winter temperature from November to April is 41·8° F. The rainfall is about 16 inches from September to April, three quarters of which falls before January.

Meran possesses a dry, cold winter climate, with a decided absence of wind, and

a large proportion of sunny days, but the
spring climate is not as good in comparison,
many invalids leaving it at the end of
February or beginning of March on this
account. Many phthisical patients reap
considerable benefit from the dry, cold and
bracing winter; an intermediate climate
between that of the Riviera, and that of
the Alpine districts.

The grape cure is carried out in the
autumn, and as this treatment is supposed
to be applicable to a large number of different complaints, the grapes have to be taken
in different quantities and at different times,
according to the disease, and to the effect to
be produced. In phthisis only one to two
pounds of grapes are to be taken daily after
breakfast, the grapes having a large amount
of sugar in them, are in this quantity said
to be nourishing and fattening. In other
complaints five or even six pounds are
ordered to be consumed daily, and a painful
task it becomes for a very dubious benefit.

Algiers.

Though Algiers is not in Europe, and though I have no knowledge of it from personal experience, yet a few words as to the place it holds as a health resort and the character of its climate may be useful.

It is very picturesquely situated on the slope of the coast range of hills facing the Mediterranean, and though the life in the town is most interesting to the visitor, owing to the various costumes and customs of the various nationalities living there, yet the city itself is not fit for invalids to reside in, on account of its insanitary conditions. But some of the suburbs, notably that of Mustapha Supérieur, situated on higher ground, and some little distance from the town, are exempt from such drawbacks, and the above suburb possesses some well placed hotels, villas and pensions.

There are great discrepancies in the various accounts of the climate, the truth probably being that winter seasons vary considerably, and that the observers have not studied the climate sufficiently long to come to a correct estimate of the average winter conditions.

The mean winter temperature is probably about 57° F. (though it has been given as high as 62° F.), and is therefore about 6° F. warmer than the Riviera. Snow lies on the mountains to as low a level as 1600 feet, and although the thermometer very rarely falls to the freezing point, people describe the atmosphere during wet weather as peculiarly damp and chilly.

The Sirocco, which is dreaded on account of its heat and dryness, as well as from its being laden with fine dust from the Sahara, is said to blow on an average on four or five days in each month; but the prevailing winds are the W. and the N.W., which are charged with vapour from the Atlantic and Mediterranean. Hence they deposit a large amount of rain and snow on the Atlas range of mountains, and Algiers itself receives about 36 inches of rain per annum, 31 inches of which fall during the winter on 90 days.

It seems doubtful whether the climate of

Algiers itself possesses for the majority of cases any superiority over the Riviera. It has advantages for some patients, namely, that it is rather warmer, that it is more equable, and that there is not the same contrast between the hot sun and the cool shade; but these advantages are rather neutralised by its being occasionally damp and cold, and on the other hand, very dusty in dry weather.

On the Northern littoral of the Mediterranean, on the contrary, when cold it is generally a dry cold, and when damp it is warm, and it is well known that it is the damp cold which is injurious to the invalid. The climate often injuriously affects those who are subject to hepatic derangements, and invalids subject to such complaints should avoid Algiers. Dr. Marcet remarks of the climate, that " it will prove inefficient in the cure of consumption."

AMERICA (U.S.).

This immense country of course comprehends a vast variety of climate, and new health resorts of more or less suitability are being yearly opened up. The moist warm climate of Florida, the dry mountain climate of Colorado, and the dry marine climate of Southern California, are the best known to English physicians.

Florida possesses a moist warm climate and has recently been recommended for certain cases of phthisis, such as would in Europe be sent to Madeira, and its climate much resembles that of the West Indian Islands. It is not very healthy during the summer months as fevers are then apt to occur.

Colorado.

The climate of Colorado and its health resorts are perhaps better known in England than any in the States, chiefly through the writings of Dr. Denison. The whole area of the State, indeed, can be reckoned as a health resort, but the places best known are Denver, Colorado Springs, and Manitou.

Colorado has a remarkably dry climate, as might have been expected from its position in the centre of a large continent, a thousand miles away in a direct line from the nearest seaboard. Changes of temperature are very sudden at times, and owing to its elevation on the central table-land of America it has a dry cold winter climate. On account of its great dryness, patients make up parties for camping out on the mountains during the summer months, and can thus live in the open air day and night. The air is certainly most invigorating even during the hot summer weather, but the winter climate is considered the special time for the cure of phthisis, just as in the Alpine resorts. During the winter there is very much less snow but considerably more wind than at Davos Platz, and it is not so cold, the coldest month being about 12° F. higher; but very severe cold is occasionally experienced.

Denver is a large and populous town, situated at an elevation of 5,200 feet, on a bare and open plain about thirteen miles eastwards from the base of the mountains, quite unprotected from cold winds in winter, and exceedingly dusty in summer. In fact, it did not appear to me to be a very suitable place for patients already attacked with disease, unless in the first stage and physically strong, although it may be very good for those who have merely a predisposition to phthisis.

The mean annual temperature for five years, from 1872-1877, was 48·6° F. ; the mean temperature for December and January 32° F.; for July 72·5° F.; the mean daily range was 28° F. The rainfall amounted to 16·15 inches, falling on 68 days, 40 of which were snowy. The annual relative humidity is only 47·2 per cent., which it will be noticed is remarkably low, while that for the Alpine regions is decidedly high.

Colorado Springs has been so named, not because it has any mineral springs of its own, but because it is near the springs of Manitou, and as it has been laid out for the purposes of a health resort, it perhaps gives it a more attractive name. It is situated on an open plain about eighty miles south of Denver, and five or six miles away from the base of the Rocky mountains, at an elevation of 5,775 feet. When I visited it there were only a few scattered houses, but it has grown very rapidly of late years, and it is said now to possess many good hotels and boarding houses.

There can be but little shelter in winter from cold winds, as it is completely exposed in every direction excepting westwards, on which side is the grand and lofty range of the Rocky Mountains, with the mighty Pike's Peak rising exactly opposite. There are many most interesting excursions in the neighbourhood, some of which, such as the ascent of Pike's Peak, one of the highest points of the Rocky Mountains, 14,400 feet, involve a considerable amount of fatigue. That, however, did not at that time, I am happy to say, stand in my way, and to the top of it I climbed. There is also a more circuitous road by which the ascent can be made with comparative ease on horseback in two days, as there is an important Government Signal and Meteorological Station at the summit. Extraordinary electrical phenomena are sometimes experienced, and so highly is everything charged with electricity that sparks can be drawn from any object.

Glen Eyrie, the Garden of the Gods, Monument Park, Manitou, and other interesting places can also be visited.

Manitou is situated about 500 feet higher than Colorado Springs, viz., at an elevation of 6,315 feet, just at the very base of the mountains. It is decidedly the most inviting of the health resorts, and being placed in a glen, and so close under the mountains, it is certainly more protected from cold winds, but at the same time does not receive so much sun. There are some good hotels but the village is quite small. The position is exceedingly beautiful, both from its wildness and rocky beauty, as well as from the luxuriance of the vegetation softening down the ruggedness of the rocks.

Here are also the mineral springs above referred to, which have given the name to Colorado Springs. There are five or six springs varying in their nature, some are highly charged with carbonic acid, one being chalybeate, and some are said to resemble those of Ems.

The district has grown rapidly in public favour since I was there, but I felt at the time that with the aid of the various springs it must become a national watering place, so good and healthy is the position, so invigorating is the air, so beautiful are the surroundings, and so many are the natural attractions of the locality, and of the excursions that may be taken therefrom.

CALIFORNIA.

The greater part of this State has little to recommend it to the health seeker; the coast line is for the most part subject to strong cool sea breezes, which are often laden with sea fog, but these winds are tempered and the fogs dispersed by passing over the coast range of hills.

A very different climate is then obtained between these mountains and the Sierra Nevada range; one where rain often does not fall for eight months together, where cultivation has to be carried on by irrigation for a great period of the year, where the heat during the summer is most intense, not unfrequently exceeding 100° F. in the shade, and where the dust is overpowering. This central plain of California no doubt gave the State its name, for it is said to be derived from two Spanish words "Caliente fornalo," meaning "a heated furnace," and well it deserves the name. There is, however, a portion of the Southern Californian littoral which is said to possess a very favourable marine climate for phthisical patients. It is remarkable in that, though a marine climate, it is dry, and does not possess that large amount of humidity of the air which is usually associated with such climates.

The best known of the resorts situated in this portion of California are Los Angeles, Santa Barbara and San Diego. The heat of the summer is tempered by the sea breezes, and is seldom excessive; while the winter temperature is very temperate, though slight frosts are occasionally experienced. The mean daily range of temperature is high. These places, indeed, possess an invigorating, dry, though not very equable, marine climate, and very good results are said to have been obtained there in phthisis; but probably the climate would be found more trying by sensitive invalids than is generally admitted.

San Francisco itself has a trying climate for those who have any delicacy of the chest, and it also cannot be considered a healthy town even in other respects. Oaklands, on the opposite side of the harbour, and the most important residential suburb of San Francisco, possesses a much more pleasant and desirable climate, in that it is exempt to a great degree from the cold sea winds, the damp sea fogs, and from the clouds of dust which trouble that city.

AUSTRALIA AND NEW ZEALAND.

In these days when travelling for health is so much the fashion, and when such magnificent Ocean Steamers have so shortened the passage, a run to Australia and New Zealand is thought merely a holiday trip for those in health, or for the jaded worker; though it still possesses and must always do so, in spite of every comfort that can be supplied, even on the best steamers, many trials for the delicate.

Consequent upon the number of those passing backwards and forwards, a more or less definite knowledge of the conditions of life in those far off colonies is spreading amongst all classes in Great Britain; yet it is still scarcely realised, how various are the climates that these countries present, and how important it is, for those who are starting for these colonies, to have some fairly definite idea as to the conditions they will there meet with, and as to the most suitable localities for their several maladies. This choice will depend on the time of their arrival, and whether their intention is to settle in one of the colonies, or merely to pay them a visit of longer or shorter duration according to medical advice. It must be borne in mind, that there are many districts and climates of both Australia and New Zealand which are not suitable for the phthisical, whether in an early stage of the disease or not; and that if a residence is taken up in any one of the large Capitals, and clerk's work or other business be undertaken which will prevent an open air life, it will be found in a large proportion of cases that very little benefit is obtained, and that they will fare no better than at home. For such work too, it must be remembered that there is almost as much competition as in England, and that he who cannot do a full day's work cannot compete with a healthy man in any employment. Again, for the more pronounced cases who have gone chiefly for the voyage, the hotels do not afford the accommodation and attendance an invalid requires; even in the large cities the hotels are not first rate, and are very inferior and a great contrast to those in the United States. As it is universally found that consumptive patients do better in their own house or apartments, than even in the best managed hotels of Europe, it is far better that they should have their own house and attendants (though colonial servants are a real and practical difficulty) if their determination is to stay for some time in the country for the benefit to be obtained from the climate. There is not then, the same temptation to join in the more or less harmful amusements of hotel life, and though the food of a hotel may be good and all that

is required for the strong, it may be quite
unfitted for the requirements of an invalid.
Far better still, as the cities are not suitable
for such cases, let the patient go to some
squatter's station up country, if he is sufficiently strong, and live there an open air life,
interesting himself as far as possible in the
pursuits of those around him.

Australia has a hot and dry climate giving
it quite a distinct character from that of
England or New Zealand. Except along
the coast regions, water-famines are not
rare and thousands of sheep and cattle may
perish in a dry season for want of water.
This remarkable dryness, however, is very
favourable to many cases of phthisis, and it
is these dry regions beyond the Blue Mountains, the Australian Alps and the Dividing
Range, which afford the most satisfactory
stations for the cure of this disease. The
death-rate from phthisis in these pastoral
regions and rural districts is less than half
that of the large cities of Australia, which
have now nearly as high a death-rate from
this disease as England.

There are three distinct climatic regions

in the colonised part of Australia. Firstly,
the coast regions and that part of the continent which is under oceanic influence and
which comprise all the Capitals of the
various colonies; secondly, the mountainous regions of Victoria, New South Wales
and Queensland; and thirdly, the dry inland
pastoral plains which extend towards the
interior of the continent, on the further side
of these mountains.

Victoria possesses all the above climates.
In Gippsland it has the best marine climate
of Australia, and in Mount Macedon, easily
reached from Melbourne, it possesses a good
mountain station with an elevation of over
3,000 feet. Its situation is so healthy and
so beautiful that it is a favourite summer
resort with the inhabitants of Melbourne.

Perhaps, however, for those with any
phthisical tendency, the dry inland plains of
the Murray district are the most satisfactory.

The large and flourishing town of
Melbourne suffers much from sudden fluc-
tuations of temperature, from cold Southerly
winds and also from the hot winds from the

interior, or so called " Brick-fielders."
These winds are extremely parching in their
nature like the " blast from a furnace ;" the
thermometer rises from 100° F. to 110° F. in
the shade during their continuance, and
recedes but little during the night ; all vegetation is parched and withered up, and the
air is laden with dust from the plains of the
interior of the continent, so that all doors
and windows have to be kept shut, and
people go out as little as possible during the
three or four days over which they usually
last.

The mean annual temperature is 57·7° F.
and the average rainfall is 25·65 inches.
During seventeen years, the temperature in the shade was registered above
100° F. on sixty-one days, and on fifty-two
occasions below 32° F.

New South Wales.—This, the oldest of the
Australian settlements, possesses all three of
the climates above spoken of, but the marine
climate as found in Sydney, Port Macquarie,
Eden, etc., though more equable than that
of Melbourne, is not very satisfactory ;
but Paramatta (the original seat of the

Government of New South Wales), Windsor,
etc., which are not immediately on the coast,
possess a rather drier and less relaxing
climate.

In Mount Victoria the colony possesses a
good highland station; and the Darling
and Murrumbidgee River districts—inland
pastoral plains—afford many more or less
satisfactory places, such as Hay, for the
stronger class of cases who can " rough it "
a little. These districts are characterised
by great heat, dryness, and remarkable
absence of cloud.

Sydney itself, situated on the south side
of its lovely and world renowned harbour,
has a more equable and at the same time
damper and more relaxing climate than that
of Melbourne or Adelaide. The hot winds
are, however, less trying and less frequent
than in those Capitals, and the winter
climate is very pleasant and healthy. The
mean annual temperature is 63° F. (winter
54·6° F., spring 63·4° F., summer 70·9° F.,
autumn 64° F.) the winter temperature
rarely falls below 40° F. The mean annual
rainfall amounts to about 50 inches.

Queensland.—The climate of Brisbane, the capital, and that of the coast generally is not considered good for phthisical patients, being oppressively moist and hot ; but in the highland district of the Darling Downs, Queensland possesses a really good climate for chest complaints, and Warwick, only about 150 miles from Brisbane, is highly spoken of as a Sanatorium.

The mean annual temperature of Brisbane is 68·7° F.

South Australia.—Adelaide the capital is exceedingly hot during the summer months, and the hot winds, above mentioned, are often very trying ; it is at that season quite unfitted for phthisical patients. It has, however, a good winter climate. The mean annual temperature is 63° F. (winter 53·2° F., spring 62° F., summer 73° F., and autumn 64° F.). The mean daily range is high, *i.e.*, 20·7° F. The temperature may vary from the extremes of 115° F. in the summer, to 33° F. in the winter.

The mean annual humidity is 58 per cent.

Tasmania.

The old name of this pretty little island was Van Dieman's land. It lies about a hundred miles off the coast of Victoria, and forms a favourite summer resort for the Australians, who are driven away from their cities by the great heat then experienced.

" Hedgerows of hawthorn and privet, unknown upon the Australian continent, abound, and the odour of sweet briar, honeysuckle and apple-blossom. There is a verdure on the hills, a softness in the air, a sense of tranquillity and repose, grateful to the traveller after the parched plains of Victoria and the glare and bustle of Melbourne."

The two principal towns in the island are Launceston on the North, and Hobart Town the capital, on the South side of the island, 121 miles apart, but now united not only by the excellent old and convict made road, but also by a railway.

Hobart Town is beautifully situated on the estuary of the river Derwent, with mount Wellington rising to a height of

4000 feet immediately behind the town. It has a very English appearance and possesses a well wooded public park called the "Domain," with prettily laid out gardens on the banks of the estuary.

The climate of Tasmania is decidedly cooler and damper than that of Australia, the mean annual temperature of Hobart Town is 55° F., and that of the coldest month (January) 50° F., equivalent to the winter temperature of the Riviera. The rainfall is 23·5 inches. Hobart Town is decidedly cooler than Launceston, and is more subject to sudden changes and cold Southerly winds; but it does not suffer so much from the hot Northerly Australian ones, which are not unfrequently felt on the north side of the island. But the Northern aspect of the island seems on the whole to be the most appropriate for chest complaints, only there is little accommodation to be had outside Launceston. During the Australian summer the island affords an excellent change of climate, but its efficacy as a permanent resort for phthisical patients seems scarcely proved.

New Zealand consists of two principal islands separated by Cook's Straits about fifteen miles wide, and lying about 1100 miles South South-East of Australia. Though New Zealand has only an average breadth of 140 miles, it extends for 1100 miles in length, or through nearly thirteen degrees of latitude. Each island now has several fine cities, such as Christchurch, Dunedin and Nelson in the South island, while Wellington the capital, Napier and Auckland, are the principal towns in the North island.

The Maoris, the native inhabitants of New Zealand, are a most interesting race, and very different from the low type of the aborigines of Australia or Tasmania, but they are fast dying out; there are now only about 40,000 in the North island, and 2000 in the South island. They are a fine, tall, well-developed race, and easily adapt themselves to civilised ways; the tattooing on some of the old chiefs is very elaborate,

but is now little practised. Their great
failing was cannibalism, though in other
respects they were greatly superior to many
savage races. The tribes were frequently
at war amongst themselves, and they used
invariably to eat their prisoners. I have
myself picked up many human bones out of
the sand heaps, charred and burnt from one
of these orgies, which took place a few miles
north of Christchurch, after a defeat and
massacre of the South islanders by one of
the Northern tribes. But one cannot here
enter into the many points of interest concerning this fine race of men, or the many
beauties of their country, with its remarkable volcanic region, where till lately the
lovely and unique pink and white terraces
of Rotomahana delighted the visitor; with
its magnificent evergreen forests, teeming
with ferns from the delicate Todea superba
to the giant tree-ferns thirty or forty feet in
height, each frond some fifteen feet in length;
with its remarkable parasitic plant the Rata,
which begins its most wonderful life by being
swallowed as a seed and then growing in
the interior of a caterpillar, and after killing

its first host begins its scarcely less curious
arboreal existence, when clinging at first to
a noble forest tree for support, it finally not
only kills but supplants it, standing at
last as an independent giant of the forest
a hundred feet or more in height.

Owing to the number of degrees of latitude
through which New Zealand extends, the
climate naturally varies very much; it is on
the whole an exceedingly good one and there
are few, if any, in the world that can compare with it in suitability for the Anglo-
Saxon race. The heat is never excessive
in the summer or the cold very great in
winter, fogs are rare, and there is much
more good settled weather than in England;
indeed it might be described as a greatly
improved edition of our own English climate.

As to temperature, Auckland is naturally
the warmest town, with a mean annual temperature of 59° F.; and Dunedin is the
coldest with a mean temperature of 50·5° F.
Wellington and Nelson are intermediate,
with a temperature of 55·5° F., and Christchurch has a mean of 52·7° F. Frosts rarely

occur anywhere in the North island, but
sharp frosts are experienced at Dunedin and
Christchurch, and severe cold and heavy
falls of snow occur on the mountains of
Westland. The rainfall and humidity differ
greatly, the rainfall varying, for instance,
from 25˙33 inches, falling on 107 days at
Christchurch on the East of the Southern island, to 119˙11 inches at Hokitika on the West
coast. Wellington seems to have the lowest
relative humidity, namely, 68 per cent., and
Hokitika the highest, 90 per cent. New
Zealand is, as a whole, subject to strong
winds and heavy gales. Wellington has the
reputation of being the worst in this respect,
though the whole Westerly coast, especially
of the South island, is much subject to heavy
Westerly gales. Of local winds the only
ones requiring notice are the hot N.W.
winds which occasionally sweep across the
fertile Canterbury plains. These winds are
probably not the same as the Australian hot
winds, as has been suggested, but are produced by the local and physical conditions
of the country. The Westerly winds in passing over the high chain of mountains along

the West coast are rendered cool and made to deposit their moisture, they then descend upon the Canterbury plains to the East of the mountains and in descending become capable of absorbing much more moisture, and therefore feel hot and dry.

Napier in the North, and Nelson in the South island (though the latter has the heavy rainfall of 81 inches) are generally considered the most suitable localities for phthisical patients. Auckland is rather humid and enervating, Wellington too windy and variable, and Dunedin too damp and raw for such patients. On the whole, Australia probably presents more suitable climates for chest cases than New Zealand, excepting during the heat of the summer.

*   *   *   *

In conclusion, I would urge on my *medical* readers the vital importance of duly weighing the constitutional condition of the patient as well as the mere local manifestation of the disease, and to take into careful consideration the previous history of the case, before deciding on sending a phthisical patient to brave the trials of a sea voyage, the rigors of an Alpine winter, or the inferior accommodation and various deficiencies of some much lauded health resort. For having myself travelled both when in health and as an invalid, I know full well how untoward occurrences (such as being becalmed in the tropics for a week, or being snowed up in an hotel without fuel for a few days during an Alpine winter), which would have seemed mere trifles in the former condition, become serious matters in the latter.

Again, I would urge on any of my *non-medical* readers, who may be fellow sufferers with myself, to take their health in hand at the very first manifestation of the disease, and to make any sacrifice necessary for a complete change of life and surroundings, till their health is completely re-established.

A few months change with careful treatment at the commencement of the disease, is often worth years of care afterwards; indeed its importance is even greater than that, for it may result in a complete cure, whereas afterwards mere palliation may only be obtainable.

Do not endeavour to struggle on a little longer "just till the end of the season," or "just till this examination is passed," and so on, for by that time this insidious disease may have gained such a hold on the constitution that the cure will take far longer to be accomplished, even if it is ever effected. Again, when once the change is decided upon, wherever it may be to, do not imagine that because the evil seems slight at first, you can do as others around you are doing ; or that you have only a " little delicacy of the chest " which will get well of itself without trouble and care on your part; for change of climate is only a means to an end, it affords no specific for the cure of this disease in the sense of the advertising quack.

Though consumption kills its thousands annually, and stands as one of the chief causes of death in most civilised countries, yet it *is* curable, but only by care and the adoption of a thoroughly healthy mode of life; so despondency should not take possession of any one so afflicted.

When recovery is so far effected and so little trace is left even on medical examination that you are pronounced cured, great care in many ways is still necessary; for cured you may be as far as the mere physical signs are concerned, yet not so as regards the constitutional discrasia.

Again and again has it been my lot to see and hear of such cases, where a foolish excursion involving excessive fatigue, or a chill, has brought on a serious relapse, perhaps never to be recovered from; for the constitution seems to require a much longer period than is generally supposed necessary to regain its normal power of resistance. But it seems impossible for a large proportion of patients to benefit by the melancholy experience of others. If, however, the few hints I have been able to give in the foregoing pages, and the advice I have attempted to offer may enable anyone to profit by my personal experiences, the author will feel his labour will not have been in vain.

INDEX.

R

SELECTED LIST OF BOOKS

IN

GENERAL LITERATURE,

PUBLISHED BY H. K. LEWIS,

136 *GOWER STREET, LONDON, W.C.*

ESTABLISHED, 1844.

*DWELLING-HOUSES, THEIR SANITARY CON-*STRUCTION AND ARRANGEMENTS. By W. H. CORFIELD, M.A., M.D. Oxon., F.R.C.P. Lond., Professor of Hygiene and Public Health at University College, London; Medical Officer of Health and Public Analyst for St. George's, Hanover Square. Second Edition, with Illustrations, cr. 8vo, 3s. 6d.

GENERAL CONTENTS.—Situation and Construction of Houses—Soils—Walls—Chimneys—Floors—Wall Coverings—Ventilation, Lighting and Warming—Overcrowding—Ventilation by Chimneys, by Windows, by Special Apparatus—Cowls—Gasburners—Stoves—Hot-water Apparatus—Water Supply—Sources of Water—Distribution—Constant Service—Filters—Removal of Refuse Matter—Dust—Cesspools—Conservancy Systems—Dry Earth System—Water Carriage System—Sewerage—Main Sewers—House Sewers—Traps—Ventilation and Drains—Water-closets, Sinks and Baths—Various kinds of Closets—Waste Pipes—Valves and Cisterns—Soil Pipes.

"This is one of the best handbooks we have met with on the subject of house sanitation . . . . . . It is a work deserving the studies of all householders who care for their own health and for that of their families." *The Lancet.*

"We do not know that there is any other book, which deals so concisely and yet so thoroughly with one of the great problems of sanitary science."—*Municipal Review.*

THE HEALTH OF CHILDREN.

By ANGEL MONEY, M.D., B.S., M.R.C.P., Assistant Physician to the Hospital for Sick Children, and to University College Hospital, etc. Crown 8vo, 6d.

"It is written in simple language, and the information which is concisely put, is just that which is required by every one who has the care of young children . . . . . . Every mother should possess a copy of this excellent treatise, and its small price (*Sixpence*) places its within the reach of all."—*Saturday Review.*

A COMPENDIUM OF DOMESTIC MEDICINE AND

COMPANION TO THE MEDICINE CHEST: Intended as a source of easy reference for Clergymen, Master Mariners, and Travellers; and for Families resident at a distance from professional assistance. By JOHN SAVORY, Member of the Society of Apothecaries, London. Tenth Edition, small 8vo, 5s.

HYDROPHOBIA: a Review of Pasteur's Treat-

ment. By W. COLLIER, M.A., M.D. Cantab., M.R.C.P., Physician to the Radcliffe Infirmary, Oxford. Crown 8vo, 6d.

HARROGATE AND ITS WATERS: Notes on the

Climate of Harrogate, and on the Chemistry of the Mineral Springs. By G. OLIVER, M.D., M.R.C.P. Crown 8vo, with Map of the Wells. 2s. 6d.

"Dr. Oliver's work is a very complete and useful one."—*Practitioner.*

ON DIET AND REGIMEN IN SICKNESS AND

HEALTH, and on the Interdependence and Prevention of Diseases and the Diminution of their Fatality. By HORACE DOBELL, M.D., Consulting Physician to the Royal Hospital for Diseases of the Chest, &c. Seventh Edition, 8vo, 10s. 6d.

GENERAL CONTENTS.—Preliminary Remarks—Rules for Promoting and Maintaining Vigorous Health in Adults Living in the Climate of the United Kingdom—Food, Heat, and Motion—Normal Diet and Regimen of Children—On the Wholesomeness and Digestibility of Various Articles of Food, and on the Modes of Cooking in Common Use—Some Principles of Diet in Disease—Fat—Fermented Liquors —Special Recipes, Directions and Appliances for the Sick-Room— Disinfection — Interdependence of Diseases — Anæmia — Fatty Degeneration—Abnormal Physiological States.

THE MANAGEMENT OF ATHLETICS IN PUBLIC

SCHOOLS. A paper read before the Medical Officers of Schools Association. By GEORGE FLETCHER, M.D. CANTAB., of Highgate ; late Medical Officer of Albert College, Framlingham, and Scholar of Clare College, Cambridge. 8vo, 1s.

"The pamphlet is one which parents and masters and medical men may all study with profit."—*Practitioner.*

ROYAT (Les Bains) IN AUVERGNE, ITS MINERAL

WATERS AND CLIMATE. By G. H. BRANDT, M.D. Crown 8vo, with Frontispiece and Map, 2s. 6d.

"We can recommend Dr. Brandt's work to those who wish for information on the waters of Royat."—*London Medical Record.*

THE LEAMINGTON WATERS CHEMICALLY,

THERAPEUTICALLY, AND CLINICALLY CONSIDERED; with Observations on the Climate of Leamington.   By FRANCIS WILLIAM SMITH, M.D. Second Edition, crown 8vo, with Illustrations, 1s. *nett.*

"We commend the book to the attention both of doctors and patients."—*The Times.*

"Dr. Smith's book will be found useful by all who meditate a visit to Leamington, and by those who are hesitating regarding the choice of a suitable resort."—*Health.*

"We trust that Dr. Smith's little treatise, written in a lively and popular style, will contribute to the very desirable end of bringing patients back to Leamington—a very useful medical guide."—*London Medical Record.*

A MANUAL OF ELEMENTARY KNOWLEDGE.

By J. OBERLIN HARRIS, M.A.   With Maps, post 4to, 3s. 6d.

"Accurate and up to date, concise and well-arranged, its explanations are short and to the point, and its methods generally simple and rational."—*School Guardian.*

LEWIS'S POCKET MEDICAL VOCABULARY.

32mo, roan, 3s. 6d.

"It may be commended to the notice, not only of the profession, but also of any one whose reading brings technical words to his notice with any frequency."—*Literary World.*

RECEIPTS FOR FLUID FOODS.

By MARY BULLAR and J. F. BULLAR, M.B. CANTAB., F.R.C.S.   16mo, 1s.

DISINFECTANTS AND HOW TO USE THEM.

By E. T. WILSON, B.M. Oxon., F.R.C.P. Lond., Physician to the Cheltenham General Hospital and Dispensary. In packets of one dozen, price 1s.

*** These cards will be found particularly suitable for heads of families, clergymen, and nurses: or for distribution among the artisans and tradesmen of our larger towns.

"They should be widely circulated by philanthropic persons and sanitarians."—*The Metropolitan.*

"These cards should be in the possession of all medical practitioners; clergymen, and others, whose duty and desire it is to prevent, as much as possible, the spread of contagious diseases."—From Dr. Lionel Beale's Work on *Disease Germs*, 1872, p. 298.

"This little card is one of the most valuable aids in the diffusion of health knowledge that we remember to have seen. Clergymen, and all others interested in the welfare of the people, could not do a wiser thing than distribute them broadcast."—*Health.*

THE PARENT'S MEDICAL NOTE BOOK.

Compiled by A. DUNBAR WALKER, M.D., C.M. Oblong post 8vo, cloth, 1s. 6d.

*** The present little work is compiled for the express object of enabling parents to keep a record of the diseases their children have passed through.—Preface.

"A record which would be of the utmost value to medical men. We heartily recommend this note-book to the use of parents."—*Health.*

"Head masters of public schools might very wisely insist upon their new pupils being provided with such a record."—*London Medical Record.*

THE METAPHYSICAL ASPECT OF NATURAL

HISTORY. A lecture by STEPHEN MONCKTON, M.D., F.R.C.P. Second Edition, with Illustrations, crown 8vo, 2s.

ILLUSTRATED LECTURES ON AMBULANCE

WORK. By R. LAWTON ROBERTS, M.D., M.R.C.S. Copiously illustrated, Third Edition, crown 8vo, 2s. 6d.

"The descriptions are in clear intelligible language, and there is a laudable absence of those long-sounding words with which we too often meet in lectures which are intended to be popular."—*Lancet.*

"Among works of this class Dr. Lawton Roberts' deserves a high place. All his descriptions are clear, he dwells upon the points of importance, and omits every detail which does not add to the precise instruction he wishes to convey. Every part of the book is good. The lucid text is made clearer still by well-chosen and well-drawn wood-cuts, and in the 164 pages scarcely a superfluous sentence is to be found." *Athenæum.*

" We can, with every confidence, advise the perusal and study of Dr. Roberts' little volume."—*Health.*

"This is a thoroughly practical and useful little book."—*Volunteer Service Gazette.*

"The directions given are clear and succinct, and we feel sure that a careful study of this little book would fit any person of ordinary intelligence to render first aid to the sick and wounded."—*Record.*

"The book is plentifully illustrated, and seems excellently adapted to its purpose."—*Spectator.*

" One of the best books on the subject that we have met with . . . . . . especially adapted for those who live in the country."—*Guardian.*

" We heartily commend the little volume to all, and especially to those engaged about our great mills and machine works, where accidents are frequent, in which timely intelligent aid would prove invaluable."—*Mechanical World.*

OSBORN'S AMBULANCE LECTURES: *Nursing.*

By SAMUEL OSBORN, F.R.C.S., Assistant-Surgeon Hospital for Women, Surgeon Royal Naval Artillery Volunteers. With Illustrations. Fcap. 8vo, 1s. 6d.

"A most useful handbook . . . . . . A series of ambulance lectures, full of sound and practical advice, not only for members of ambulance classes, but for all to whose lot may fall the care of a sick room."—*Society.*

COMPANION VOLUME BY THE SAME AUTHOR.

OSBORN'S AMBULANCE LECTURES: *First Aid.*

Fcap. 8vo, 1s. 6d.

"Two handy little volumes . . . . . . give compactly, and in small space, information as useful in the home as in the hospital."—*The Graphic.*

"Well adapted for the purpose."—*The Lancet.*

DIAGRAMS FOR LECTURERS TO AMBULANCE

Classes and for Popular Lectures on Physiology. *Prospectus on application.*

SON REMEMBER. *An Essay on the Discipline of*

the Soul beyond the Grave. By the REV. JOHN PAUL, B.A., Rector of St. Alban's, Worcester. Crown 8vo, 3s. 6d.

"His tone is devout, he has no craving after novelty for its own sake . . . . he has in Chapter V., 'What is written,' some sensible remarks on the way of interpreting scripture."—*The Academy.*

TEST QUESTIONS ON THE LATIN LANGUAGE.

By F. W. LEVANDER, F.R.A.S., Classical Master in University College, London.   Cr. 8vo, 2s.

"A good feature of the work is the immense variety from which the judicious teacher can make a selection suitable to the class of boys that may be under his care."—*Schoolmaster.*

"Many of them are original, others have been taken from various examination papers; altogether they furnish so great an abundance of "tests" of all degrees of difficulty, that the student who can answer the majority of them need have no fear as to the results of any ordinary paper in Latin."—*School Guardian.*

By the same Author.

SOLUTIONS OF THE QUESTIONS IN MAGNETISM

AND ELECTRICITY.   Set at the Intermediate Science and Preliminary Scientific Pass Examinations of the University of London, 1860-1884, together with Definitions, Dimensions of Units, Miscellaneous Examples, etc.   Second Edition, fcap. 8vo, 2s. 6d.

"Undoubtedly a useful book, it gives a good idea of what is required by the examiners."—*English Mechanic.*

"It will doubtless prove of great service to many candidates. Mr. Levander appears to us to have answered the questions at once correctly and concisely."—*Lancet.*

"Mr. Levander may be congratulated on his unpretending, but exceedingly useful little book. The answers given are models of conciseness and accuracy, and show the student exactly how questions should be answered."—*Education.*

QUESTIONS ON HISTORY AND GEOGRAPHY, Set

at the Matriculation Examination of the University of London, 1844-1886. Second Edition, fcap. 8vo, 2s.

" Mr. Levander has arranged and classified the papers with care and judgment."—*School and University Magazine.*

"Any one who will conscientiously follow out this plan will find any compilation of questions such as this invaluable."—*The Practical Teacher.*

"This is a useful compilation."—*School Guardian.*

BY THE SAME EDITOR.

QUESTIONS ON THE ENGLISH LANGUAGE, Set

at the Matriculation Examinations of the University of London, 1858-1885. Fcap. 8vo, 2s. 6d.

"Besides being useful for its own special purpose, the volume will be serviceable to all students and teachers of English, for there are no more instructive and suggestive hints on points of English syntax and derivation than those furnished by the London Matriculation questions."— *Schoolmaster.*

"The book will be useful for self-instruction, especially to that ever-increasing class of readers who find it impossible to take in the meaning of any printed matter unless they are questioned upon it."—*Saturday Review.*

MEDICAL FASHIONS IN THE NINETEENTH

CENTURY, including a Sketch of Bacterio-Mania and the Battle of the Bacilli. By EDWARD T. TIBBITS, M.D. Lond., Physician to the Bradford Infirmary, and to the Bradford Fever Hospital. Crown 8vo, 2s. 6d.

PHOTO-MICROGRAPHY; including a Description

of the Wet Collodion and Gelatino-Bromide Processes, together with the best Methods of Mounting and Preparing Microscopic Objects for Photo-Micrography. By A. COWLEY MALLEY, B.A., M.B., B.Ch. T.C.D. Second Edition, with Photographs and Illustrations, crown 8vo, 7s. 6d.

" Mr. Malley has done good service to science by the production of his compendious and practical treatise."—*Chemical News.*

" The veriest novice may become proficient (of course after practice) if he will study Mr. Malley's little work with care and attention."—*Knowledge.*

MATRICULATION CLASSICS, QUESTIONS AND

ANSWERS. By Rev. J. R. WALTERS, B.A., Assistant Master in University College School. Second Edition, crown 8vo, 2s. 6d.

"We can safely recommend this work as helpful to London Matriculation students."—*School and University Magazine.*

"The Questions in Classics, selected and answered by Mr. Walters, are such as involve peculiarities of accidence and construction which the student is apt to overlook in the ordinary course of his reading."—*Educational News.*

THE CONDITION OF GAOLS, HOSPITALS, AND

other Institutions as described by John Howard. By J. B. BAILEY, Librarian to the Royal Medical and Chirurgical Society. Demy 8vo, 1s.

WINES OF THE BIBLE.

By NORMAN KERR, M.D., F.L.S.   Demy 8vo, 6d.

ROUMANIAN FAIRY TALES AND LEGENDS.

Dedicated by permission to the Queen of Roumania. Translated by E. B. MAWR. With Photographs and Wood Engravings, cloth gilt, 5s.

"A set of delightful stories of an infinitely charming character."—*Fun.*

"Neatly and prettily written. They will be found both agreeable and novel, both instructive and amusing."—*Truth.*

"They are graceful specimens of their kind, ... they are adorned by a charming photograph of the Queen of Roumania."—*Athenæum.*

"In the shape of a very handsome little volume, forming a most suitable present for children, as well as a not unwelcome addition to the folk-lore shelves of older readers, we have here a translation of some of the popular Basme (tales) and legends of the country."—*From the Folk-Lore Record.*

"As delightful a book as we have seen for many a long day . . . . . . Fairy tales are always sure to please, and possessing the additional charm of freshness these stories are bound to become popular wherever they find their way . . . . . . they are one and all captivating alike : young readers, indeed—and their elders as well—owe a debt of gratitude to the lady who has translated these exquisite little stories into English with so much grace."—*The Boy's Newspaper.*

"To children, this little work, which, we may add, is got up with exquisite taste, and is embellished with a few illustrations, including a striking portrait and autograph of the first Queen of Roumania, will prove an inexhaustible fund of delight, while their elders will find in its perusal much that will throw a light upon the mode of thought and expression that prevails among the inheritors of Trajan's Dacia."—*Galignani's Messenger* (Paris).

SIMPLE INTEREST, WITH MODELS, HINTS FOR

Working, Cautions, and numerous Examples, With Answers. By REV. F. W. COWLEY, B.A., Assistant Master of University College School, London. Crown 8vo, 1s,

"The most handy volume on Simple Interest we have seen. The explanations are clear, and the illustrations exactly to the point."—*Schoolmaster.*

"There are, no doubt, many text-books of arithmetic which furnish a sufficiently clear exposition of the rules of Interest; but we know none which contains so many carefully classified exercises for practice, as this useful little work."—*Educational News.*

LEAFLETS.

THE KING'S VISIT TO THE HEART OF THE CITY.
A Parable. 1½d. each or 1s. per dozen.

GOSPEL OF THE FLOWERS.
1d. each or 6s. per 100.

MY TIMES ARE IN THY HAND.
2d. per dozen.

PUBLISHING DEPARTMENT.

MR. LEWIS undertakes the complete production of Books, Pamphlets, etc., including printing, illustrating by the best methods, binding, etc. All works entrusted to us receive the best care and attention in order to ensure accuracy and attractiveness in their get up.

Estimates, specimen book of types, and other information will be forwarded on application.

London, Printed by H. K. Lewis, 136 *Gower Street, W.C.*